Surviving the Top Ten Challenges of Software Testing

A PEOPLE-ORIENTED APPROACH

Also Available from Dorset House Publishing

The Deadline: A Novel About Project Management
by Tom DeMarco
ISBN: 0-932633-39-0   Copyright ©1997   320 pages, softcover

Exploring Requirements: Quality Before Design
by Donald C. Gause and Gerald M. Weinberg
ISBN: 0-932633-13-7   Copyright ©1989   320 pages, hardcover

Handbook of Walkthroughs, Inspections, and Technical Reviews
by Daniel P. Freedman and Gerald M. Weinberg
ISBN: 0-932633-19-6   Copyright ©1990   464 pages, hardcover

Managing Expectations: Working with People Who Want More, Better, Faster, Sooner, NOW!
by Naomi Karten   foreword by Gerald M. Weinberg
ISBN: 0-932633-27-7   Copyright ©1994   240 pages, softcover

Measuring and Managing Performance in Organizations
by Robert D. Austin   foreword by Tom DeMarco and Timothy Lister
ISBN: 0-932633-36-6   Copyright ©1996   240 pages, softcover

Peopleware: Productive Projects and Teams
by Tom DeMarco and Timothy Lister
ISBN: 0-932633-05-6   Copyright ©1987   200 pages, softcover

Quality Software Management, Vol. 4: Anticipating Change
by Gerald M. Weinberg
ISBN: 0-932633-32-3   Copyright ©1997   504 pages, hardcover

Find Out More About These and Other DH Books

Contact us to request a Book & Video Catalog and a free issue of *The Dorset House Quarterly*, or to confirm price and shipping information.

DORSET HOUSE PUBLISHING
353 West 12th Street   New York, NY 10014   USA
1-800-342-6657   212-620-4053   fax: 212-727-1044
dhpubco@aol.com   www.dorsethouse.com

SURVIVING THE TOP TEN

CHALLENGES of

SOFTWARE TESTING

A PEOPLE-ORIENTED APPROACH

William E. Perry
Randall W. Rice

DORSET HOUSE PUBLISHING
353 WEST 12TH STREET
NEW YORK, NEW YORK 10014

Library of Congress Cataloging-in-Publication Data

```
Perry, William E.
    Surviving the top ten challenges of software testing : a people
-oriented approach / William E. Perry, Randall W. Rice.
      p.   cm.
    ISBN 0-932633-38-2  (pbk.)
    1. Computer software--Testing.  I. Rice, Randall W.  II. Title.
QA76.76.T48P493  1997
005.1'4--DC21                                              97-44565
                                                              CIP
```

Trademark credits: All trade and product names are either trademarks, registered trademarks, or service marks of their respective companies, and are the property of their respective holders and should be treated as such.

Cover Design: David McClintock

Distributed in the English language in Singapore, the Philippines, and Southeast Asia by Toppan Co., Ltd., Singapore; in the English language in India, Bangladesh, Sri Lanka, Nepal, and Mauritius by Prism Books Pvt., Ltd., Bangalore, India; and in the English language in Japan by Toppan Co., Ltd., Tokyo, Japan.

Printed in the United States of America

Library of Congress Catalog Number: 97-44565

ISBN: 0-932633-38-2   12   11   10   9   8   7   6   5   4   3   2   1

ACKNOWLEDGMENTS

We would like to thank Dorset House Publishing Company for recognizing testing as more than a technical problem. That made this book a reality. A special thanks goes to David McClintock, who did a superb job in editing our text and keeping the project on track, and to Wendy Eakin for her creative input and encouragement.

We would also like to thank the many professional testers and information technology professionals who have contributed to this book by participating in surveys, providing input during our seminars, and encouraging us to address the people-oriented issues in testing. Without this input, there would have been no basis for this book.

Finally, and most importantly, we would like to thank God for allowing us to be in a unique position at a unique time to help others with the message of this book. As the authors, we believe that God is the Master Tester. In our lives, God has tested us very extensively.

WILLIAM E. PERRY, CQA, CQE, CSTE
RANDALL W. RICE, CQA, CSTE

DEDICATION

To our wives and families,
whom we have tested on many occasions.

CONTENTS

CONTENTS

viii

CONTENTS

SURVIVING THE TOP TEN CHALLENGES *of* SOFTWARE TESTING

A PEOPLE-ORIENTED APPROACH

CHAPTER ONE

HOW TESTING
TESTS TESTERS

The word *test* has multiple meanings and is interpreted in different ways by different people. It can be defined as a method or process, or as "an inquiry into the value or nature of something." This book embraces yet another definition, that a test is "an event or situation that tries a person's qualities." In other words, when we put a person, or something a person has developed—such as software—to the test, we try that person's qualities. Testing tries such qualities as patience, fairness, self-esteem, ambition, credibility, capability, and competitiveness.

Many testers find themselves in a dilemma. Their job is challenging enough in itself, but when coupled with office politics and interpersonal conflict, it can tax a tester's mental health. This book offers an action plan on how to survive political situations while developing and performing a high-quality test process.

THE TESTER'S WORLD

In the early days of information technology, the waterfall software development methodology defined in a highly structured way the point at which different types of testing had to occur to produce high-quality software. However, two conditions inhibited effective testing. The first was that while the software development component of the methodology was well defined, the testing component was not. The second condition was that because testing was the last activity in the software development process—and because projects were invariably behind schedule during development—testing was the activity most likely to be cut short to meet predefined implementation schedules.

These two conditions have shaped the tester's world during the past five decades. This book describes this world and its challenges in great detail, but for now, as a way of introducing the tester's world, let's look at some of the assumptions and attitudes commonly held about testing:

- *Testers are holding up implementation.* Often, it seems that everyone is ready to go into production, but the tests aren't complete. Someone has to be blamed, and since the testers are the last ones to give their okay prior to production, the testers are blamed for the delay.
- *The best way to beat the testers is to reduce the amount of test time available.* Many developers view testing as an us-versus-them game, in which testers nitpick and delay implementation over unimportant issues. Knowing the rigidity of implementation dates, developers may be tempted to delay testing as long as possible, so the amount of test time is reduced and the testers have less opportunity to find problems.
- *Test, then code.* Some developers invert the process by sending partially completed code into testing, expecting the testers to find the problems. This saves devel-

opers a lot of work, at least initially, enabling them to do sloppy coding and still get credit for a high-quality system—if the testers find the problems.

- *If defects get into production, it's the testers' fault.* Some developers try to isolate design from defects, so that design is considered a developer's responsibility, and defects, a tester's responsibility. When defects are encountered in production, it's the testers' problem, not the developers' problem.

- *Developers need training, testers don't.* Most developers are trained in how to design and code software, but are not trained in how to test. We have interviewed many individuals involved in testing, and they say their training is comprised of these four words: ". . . and then you test"!

Assumptions and attitudes like these ensure that the tester's world isn't always a happy one. However, it doesn't have to be that way. Testers need to take time to better understand their world and how they can change it. This starts with an understanding of the roles testers play as people.

TESTER 1 VERSUS TESTER 2

In reality, each tester must function in two disparate roles, which we will call Tester 1 and Tester 2 (see Figure 1.1). Tester 1 is a technician who plans and performs tests. Tester 2 is a politician who negotiates with individuals and the many different agendas they represent.

Tester 1 can be a happy person. Most testers know what to test and how to test. If life were that simple, the tester's world would be a delightful place to dwell, but the role Tester 2 plays is much more complex.

Tester 2 must be a politician, and must employ skill sets other than testing, such as communication, negotiation, psychology, marketing, and writing skill sets. Tester 2 operates in and must survive in the highly political corporate world.

Figure 1.1: Tester 1 and Tester 2.

Testers that only develop their Tester 1 skill sets face getting beaten up on a regular basis. Testers that emphasize Tester 2 skill sets will feel the pain of too many defects caught in production and not caught in testing.

The ideal tester maintains a balance between the roles exemplified by Tester 1 and Tester 2. The former will excel with proficient testing skills, but still needs Tester 2 skills to achieve maximum effectiveness and success. Tester 2 will help create an environment in which Tester 1 can succeed.

This book defines the ten major challenges faced by Tester 1 that cannot be solved with Tester 1 skill sets alone. The fundamental challenges Tester 1 faces in mastering Tester 2 skills are to understand why those skills are important, and to discover how to improve software testing by using them effectively.

THE ROOT CAUSE OF THE TESTER'S PEOPLE CHALLENGE

There are many variables involved in testing software, and it cannot be viewed as a single, repeatable process. The process tends to change with each software system being tested. This variable nature of testing adds significantly to the challenge of working effectively with people.

Let's examine five of the variables that affect the software testing process: the development process, the software risk, the customer/user involvement, the test process, and the skill of the testers. These are illustrated as continua in Figure 1.2.

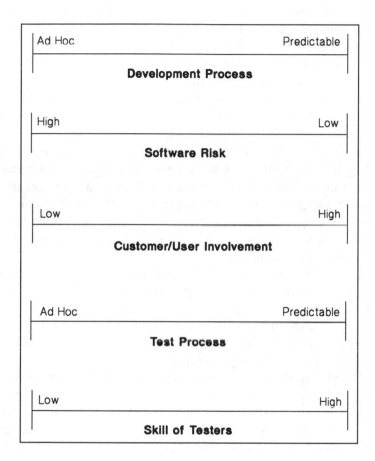

Figure 1.2: Continua of Involvement in Testing.

Software can be developed using different development processes, each at different levels of maturity ranging from an ad hoc, informal development process to a very structured, predictable process. If the process is predictable, the tester is better able to test, because the strengths and weaknesses of the development process will be known and the tester can focus test effort on the weaknesses.

The risk associated with the software being tested can rank from high to low. There are many risk models, but generally, high-risk systems include those that manage significant monetary values, those that are very important to the success of the organization, and those that are large and complex. Obviously, testers need to concentrate more effort on high-risk software than they do on low-risk software.

Research studies by the Quality Assurance Institute indicate that customer/user involvement is the single most important factor affecting the productivity of the software development process. High customer involvement leads to low-cost, high-quality software. Software developed with low customer involvement is susceptible to greater dissatisfaction, because the customer has few opportunities to interact with it during development and to suggest changes. Testers benefit from processes with high customer involvement because the systems tend to be better designed.

The test process, like the development process, can range from ad hoc and informal to highly structured and predictable. The more ad hoc the test process, the more difficulties the testers will experience in performing testing effectively. The more predictable the test process, the more the tester can rely on the process to identify problems.

The skill of the testers has a major effect on the test process. Because the process varies from system to system and is usually not prescribed in minute detail, testers must possess a certain level of professional skill. This means that the tasks an experienced tester knows need to be performed do not have to be explicitly incorporated into the defined process. However, even test processes that are written in minute detail will not be used effectively if the testers do not possess the necessary skills, or are not adequately trained.

The above discussion of five aspects of software testing is not meant to be complete, but rather, representative of the factors that affect software testing. Other factors include the extensiveness and effectiveness of tools, the budget for testing, the testing schedule, the support from management, and the motivation level of the testers.

For each software system being tested, the test factor can be placed on a continuum. For example, if the development process had matured slightly above ad hoc, then that continuum might be set at about the twenty-five percent mark. Similarly, the software risk would be set, the amount of customer/user involvement set, the type of test process would be noted on the continuum, as well as the skill of the testers.

Marking the continua in effect establishes a test footprint for the software system being tested, which can then be interpreted to indicate the potential people problems that will be associated with testing the software. Generally, the closer the footprint comes to the left-hand side of the continuum, the greater the people problem. In other words, if the footprint is aligned straight down the left side, indicating ad hoc development process, high-risk software, low customer/user involvement, ad hoc test process, and low tester skills, there is a very high probability that testers will experience people problems in testing that system.

THE TOP TEN PEOPLE-RELATED CHALLENGES

We have spent years developing testing processes, writing books and newsletters on testing, and teaching seminars on how to test. All of these have emphasized Tester 1 activities—the task of testing software. However, the toughest questions and challenges currently faced by the testers appear to be those involving their relationships with other people, the people challenges that require Tester 2 skill sets. After talking to literally hundreds of testing practitioners, we have identified ten major challenges facing testers, and all of them are people-related. We list them below in descending sequence from the number ten challenge to the single most difficult challenge facing testers. Each of the following challenges is discussed, respectively, in Chapters 3 through 12. The assessment categories correspond to the self-assessment test in Chapter 2.

Challenge #10: Getting Trained in Testing
(Assessment category: Software testing training)

Testers traditionally receive little or no testing education. The challenge the tester faces is how to test when one has never been trained in testing. Many testers were trained in the development process, and at the conclusion of that process were told, "Oh, by the way, when you're finished you need to test!" Until 1996, when the Quality Assurance Institute established a common body of knowledge for testers and an associated certification program, there had not been a commonly accepted skill set for testing. While some individuals may have a natural instinct toward testing, it is not an inborn skill. Testers are made, not born.

Challenge #9: Building Relationships with Developers
(Assessment category: Developer/tester teamwork)

In many organizations, testing is an us-versus-them mentality. The testers are often made to look like the bad guys. As long as software development projects are treated as two parts—one part development and one part testing—the us-versus-them mentality will persist. The solution to overcome this challenge is to build a team of developers and testers in which both success and failure are shared equally.

Challenge #8: Testing Without Tools
(Assessment category: Testing tools)

Testing is normally practiced as an art rather than an engineering discipline. People do what they think is necessary to test, which in many cases is very labor-intensive. Even when tools are available and the use of tools is defined in the testing process, they frequently are not integrated into the *actual* testing process. The challenge the tester faces when tools are not used is to manage and test perhaps thousands of small pieces of data. As new systems grow larger and more complex with each generation, testing without tools in today's environment is becoming logistically impossible.

Challenge #7: Explaining Testing to Managers
(Assessment category: Management involvement in software testing)

Testing has never been an activity of great interest to information system managers. Testing is looked at as something that has to be done, but not as a very creative or desirable endeavor. In some organizations, being assigned to testing is almost punishment. The manager's attitude is reflected in the disparity between the time spent with and the pay grades allocated for testers, versus those allotted to developers. Effective management cannot occur without the commitment of managers' time and budgets in testing. At one extreme, many people have spelled testing commitment "M-O-N-E-Y," because for them anything short of monetary investment is lip service.

Challenge #6: Communicating with Customers—And Users
(Assessment category: Interaction with customers and users)

This challenge identifies and differentiates between customers and users. The customer has a vested interest in testing because it is the customer who is the sponsor and the one who pays for the software; on the other hand, the user also has a vested interest as the individual using the software. However, the interest of the customer tends more toward meeting objectives and including functionality, while users are often more concerned about ease of use and the operability of the software. The testers need to know the customers and users, to encourage their involvement, and to maintain a continuous dialog with them.

Challenge #5: Making Time for Testing
(Assessment category: Budgeting and scheduling testing)

Testers are frequently placed under excessive stress when they are cast as the group that stands in the way of getting the software into production. When schedules are first established, time is allocated for testing, but developers frequently usurp that time for additional development. In addition, testing is frequently understaffed for the work load required. The solution to this major challenge is the involvement of the testers in scheduling, and the clear prioritization of what needs to be validated in testing.

Challenge #4: Testing What's Thrown Over the Wall
(Assessment category: Developer/tester communication)

Traditionally, developers and testers don't talk to each other. When the developers are finished, they throw the system "over the wall" for the testers to test. When testing is complete, the testers throw the results back. This challenge for testers is to repair communication breakdowns with developers. Effective ongoing communication between the developers and testers from the start of the project to completion will lead to higher quality on both sides of the wall.

Challenge #3: Hitting a Moving Target
(Assessment category: Building test criteria)

This challenge concerns change management. Many projects start with requirements that are not fully defined and then continually change throughout the project. When requirements change, the testers are trying to hit a moving target. In addition, the technical environment of the software testing effort may also undergo significant change during the project. The challenge testers face is to identify the revised requirements and then to modify the criteria that will perform the testing. Unless both the requirements and the test criteria or test plan are kept up to date, testers may set criteria for the wrong version of requirements.

Challenge #2: Fighting a Lose-Lose Situation
(Assessment category: Agreement on acceptable quality levels)

Testers are often put in a lose-lose situation with regard to quality. If they report that the software is not of a quality that may be placed into production, they are blamed for delays in implementation. If they certify that the software is ready for production, the typical problems that occur in production may seem to prove them wrong, and may expose them to blame. This challenge requires a clear division of responsibility between the developers and the testers for the quality and reliability of the software.

Challenge #1: Having to Say No
(Assessment category: Reliance on testers' results and opinions)

The number one people-related challenge faced by testers is telling developers and customers that the software has problems, what the problems are, the status of the software, and their recommendation on what to do with the software. When the testers are bearers of bad news, they become the enemy. The solution is to define up front the testers' role and responsibility, as well as to prescribe the way that results are presented to developers and customers, how system problems are described, and the way in which recommendations for improving the software are offered.

ROAD MAP THROUGH THE BOOK

This book is designed to assist you in addressing the people-related challenges that testers face. This three-step process will help you use the book effectively:

Step 1: Perform a self-assessment to identify your weaknesses in meeting the people-related challenges in testing. Chapter 2 is the vehicle for this self-assessment. Use it to identify your weaknesses and to relate them to the ten testing challenges.

Step 2: Learn how to improve your people challenge weaknesses. Using the results of the self-assessment, read more about the challenges in Chapters 3 through 12. The chapters describe the challenges, the solutions for the challenges, and the guidelines for implementing those solutions. Chapters 3 to 12 are each structured as follows:

1. Overview: A synopsis of the chapter is presented.
2. State of the Practice: This section illustrates the chapter's people issue with a brief case study based on the authors' experience. The scenario shows how the problem addressed by the challenge typically occurs in a testing environment.
3. Impact on Testing: This section attempts to quantify or explain the consequences of not addressing the challenge.
4. Solutions to the Challenge: This is the heart of the chapter, in which one or more solutions to overcome the challenge are laid out in step-by-step format.
5. Solution Impediments: This section raises the "what if" and "how do I" questions you may face in implementing the solutions.
6. Guidelines for Success: A series of effective steps is offered toward maximizing the progress of your solutions.
7. Plan of Action: This section provides steps to follow in solving the testing challenge.

Step 3: Build a master plan of action for improvement. Drawing on the solutions, guidelines, and plans described in Chapters 3 through 12, the final chapter outlines a tactical process for overcoming your most difficult people challenge.

At the end of this three-step process, you will have developed a profile of the people-related challenges you face in testing, and a plan of action for dealing with those challenges. Then you just need to put that plan of action in place, and to redo the self-assessment in a few months to assess changes in your testing environment.

CHAPTER TWO

DOES TESTING TEST YOU?

A line from a famous children's novel states, "If you do not know where you're going, all roads lead there!" This lesson in living is the basis of all improvement programs. If you spend your life doing routine testing tasks, and not planning how to improve your professional position, you will continue to drift for a lifetime.

This chapter provides self-assessment rating charts to help you evaluate your testing career. The assessment process is designed to serve three purposes. The first is to develop a baseline of where you are today. The second purpose is to point you to the chapters in the book that offer you the most benefit. The third purpose is to help you lay the groundwork for a plan of action for improvement, which is described in the final chapter of this book.

WHY DO A SELF-ASSESSMENT?

It's important to periodically stop in life and assess where you are. Self-assessments force you to examine and evaluate your current status. Painful as self-assessments may be, you should do them for the following reasons:

1. *Self-assessments force you to look at yourself through the eyes of the self-assessment process.* It is, in effect, an assessment from an independent party, just as a medical examination is an assessment by a physician of your physical health.
2. *Self-assessments establish a baseline for improvement.* If you are going to improve, you need to have a basis for determining whether or not improvement has been achieved. A self-assessment taken at the beginning and end of the improvement process will demonstrate change or the lack of change.
3. *Self-assessments can force you to stop being content with the status quo.* It's only natural to immerse yourself in work rather than confront a potential lack of personal progress. The self-assessment in this chapter can serve as a "reality check" that will stimulate the kind of personal improvements offered in this book.

THE THREE NECESSARY INGREDIENTS FOR SUCCESS

Success can be thought of as personal satisfaction with one's career and status in life, and this can have different meanings for different people. Put simply, if you achieve what you want to achieve, you are successful. Achieving success, however, is rarely so simple, and it requires you to do three things:

1. *Develop a personal baseline.* The baseline tells you where you are now. At the conclusion of this self-assessment, as we mentioned above, you will have established a software testing baseline for yourself.
2. *Develop a personal vision.* The vision is the set of assessment criteria that, if achieved, would match what you would rate as a success. It is not inappropriate to change your vision or goals periodically throughout your lifetime; what is important is to have a vision.

3. *Implement a plan to close the gap between your baseline and your vision.* This shortfall is frequently called a "frustration gap," because you know where you are and where you want to be, but you become frustrated that these aren't the same.

There are two ways to close the frustration gap. One is to move your vision downward toward your baseline. For example, if you currently weigh 175 pounds and have a vision of weighing 160 pounds, your frustration gap would be 15 pounds. You can close the frustration gap by deciding that you really look good at 175 pounds, and that no dieting or exercise is necessary. The second, and preferred, way to close the frustration gap is to develop and follow an action plan that will lead you from your baseline to your vision. With an awareness of your baseline and your vision, it is possible to measure your progress and to adjust your plan if necessary.

SELF-ASSESSMENT INSTRUCTIONS

The software testing self-assessment document that follows asks you to rate yourself on how well you have achieved a set of twenty people-oriented criteria. For example, the first criterion relates to the amount of formal training you have had in software. For this and the other nineteen criteria, you assess yourself in one of four categories:

- *Very adequate:* Your personal assessment of yourself is that you have fully achieved the intent of the criteria.
- *Adequate:* You have not fully achieved the intent of the criteria, but you have achieved sufficient aspects of the criteria to perform your job effectively.
- *Inadequate:* You have not achieved the intent of the criteria to the level that enables you to perform your job effectively.
- *None:* You have not yet addressed any aspect of the area covered by the assessment criteria.

Let's look at an example of how you might rate yourself for the criterion of software testing training:

- *Very adequate:* You have had sufficient training in all areas of software testing, and fully understand and feel qualified to perform a wide range of testing tasks.
- *Adequate:* You have received the training necessary to perform your current software testing job.
- *Inadequate:* You are performing aspects of your current job for which you have had no formal training.
- *None:* You have never attended a formal software training course.

At this point, assess yourself in the twenty people-oriented assessment criteria using the software tester's self-assessment instrument that follows. Please note that there is room in the assessment document for you to write about how you arrived at your assessment rating. These comments will be helpful as you build a plan of action to improve your career satisfaction.

SUMMARIZING THE SELF-ASSESSMENT RESULTS

Your next task is to summarize your responses on the Self-Assessment Summarization Worksheet, as follows:

- Develop a score for ten sets of two questions each, adding two at a time, consecutively, from one to twenty. For each set of questions, there is a minimum score of two and a maximum score of eight. Each *very adequate* scores four points, each *adequate*, three points, each *inadequate*, two points, and each *none*, one point.
- Develop a total score for the self-assessment by adding the ten two-question sets. The total score will be in the range of 20 to 80 points.

These scores should be posted on the Self-Assessment Summarization Worksheet, a sample of which immediately follows the assessment tables given on the next five pages.

Software Testers' Self-Assessment on People-Related Skill Sets.

#	ASSESSMENT CRITERIA	ASSESSMENT RATING				COMMENTS
		Very Adequate (4)	Adequate (3)	Inadequate (2)	None (1)	
1	Adequacy of the formal training that you have received in the practice of planning and performing software testing. (NOTE: Training from all sources should be evaluated, not just training provided by your current employer.)					
2	Adequacy of the formal training that you have received in the areas that support the practice and planning of software testing, such as risk analysis, software development methods, interpersonal skills, oral and written communication skills, measurement and statistical skills. (NOTE: Training from all sources should be evaluated, not just training provided by your current employer.)					
3	Adequacy of equal sharing of success and failure between the developers and testers (for example, the testers and developers are considered a single team and not two groups).					

4	Adequacy of the testers' inclusion in the entire development process; specifically, that the testers are aware of the objectives and high-level requirements for the software and have input into the design and implementation of the software.		
5	Adequacy of the tool sets available to testers before the tests are performed.		
6	Adequacy of training and support testers receive in using the set of testing tools.		
7	Adequacy of senior management's time divided between managing software development and managing software testing. (NOTE: Studies show the total development time is equally divided between development and testing, thus, one might consider this ratio a baseline for management's division of time.)		

Software Testers' Self-Assessment (Cont'd).

8	Adequacy of management's investment in the testing process, including resources spent for testing processes, tools, and training, as well as personal interest in the challenges and problems associated with testing.			
9	Adequacy of the profiles that testers have of the software's customers and users, especially concerning the specific needs of each category of customer and user.			
10	Adequacy of the software testers' interaction with all categories of customers and users, particularly of the feedback and support received from them.			
11	Adequacy of the testers' involvement in, and agreement with, the budgets and schedules established for performing software testing.			
12	Adequacy of the testers' involvement in adjusting testing schedules and budgets as they are impacted by slippages and changing requirements and slippages or changes in the developers' budgets and schedules.			

Software Testers' Self-Assessment (Cont'd).

13	Adequacy of communication, and of communication opportunities, between developers and testers to plan for and discuss test results.			
14	Adequacy of response and acceptance from developers to the test results and test recommendations made for correcting and improving the software.			
15	Adequacy of the definition of the requirements and of the design for developing the testers to validate the requirements and design criteria.			
16	Adequacy of the documentation of changes to the initial requirements and design so that testers can change or modify test criteria to validate the current software requirements and design criteria.			
17	Adequacy of the definition of the acceptable quality levels in number and type of defects related to the functional requirements, design requirements, and other related quality criteria such as ease of use, security, maintainability, and so forth.			

Software Testers' Self-Assessment (Cont'd).

18	Adequacy of the shared understanding between developers, customers, users, and management as to the quality and reliability levels expected once the software is placed into production.		
19	Adequacy of the credibility of the test process and the software testers using that process to develop an informed opinion about the software being tested and the viability of placing that software into production.		
20	Adequacy of the decisions made by developers, customers, users, and management to correct or change the software, and of the decision to place it into production.		

Software Testers' Self-Assessment (Cont'd).

Self-Assessment Summarization Worksheet.

QUESTIONS IN QUESTION SET	ASSESSMENT CATEGORY	SCORE	REFERENCE CHAPTER
1 and 2	Software testing training		3
3 and 4	Developer/tester teamwork		4
5 and 6	Testing tools		5
7 and 8	Management involvement in software testing		6
9 and 10	Interaction with customers and users		7
11 and 12	Budgeting and scheduling testing		8
13 and 14	Developer/tester communication		9
15 and 16	Building test criteria		10
17 and 18	Agreement on acceptable quality levels		11
19 and 20	Reliance on testers' results and opinions		12
	TOTAL		

INTERPRETING SELF-ASSESSMENT RESULTS

Using the results recorded on the Self-Assessment Summarization Worksheet, two conclusions can be drawn: an overall assessment and a criterion assessment. In the following sections, each possible score range is interpreted, first for your organization's overall handling of people-related issues, then for your own aptitude in each of ten criteria.

Conclusion 1: Overall Assessment

Referring to the total point score from your self-assessment, evaluate your testing environment based on the corresponding interpretation provided below.

Score   *Interpretation*

20 to 35   Judging solely from your score, you are ill-equipped to deal with the political/people issues of software testing. You probably experience very high levels of frustration with your inability to impact the development of software and the decisions made by developers, users, customers, and managers regarding the adequacy of software under development and the decisions related to putting software into production. Very significant changes need to be made in your personal development and the processes your organization uses to test software. You've come to the right place! You have the most to gain from this assessment and from this book.

36 to 50   You and your organization have the beginnings of the environment and the skill sets that will enable the testing people issues to be addressed. Much work is needed to effectively address the people problems your testers face, but the basic framework is in place.

51 to 65   Your organization's approach for addressing people-related issues in testing seems to be well developed, but is probably only partially deployed, and only preliminary results have been achieved. Conflict probably continues to exist between testers and other parties who have a vested interest in the success of the software. However, there are probably mechanisms in place that enable this conflict to be partially resolved without any long-term damage to relationships. Some additional effort in fine-tuning is necessary to achieve a world-class environment, in which testers are truly partners in the development and operation of high-quality software.

66 to 80   Your organization has either become, or should soon become, a world-class organization in integrating testing and development into a single, mutually supportive activity. Organizations at the lower end of this point scale (between 66 and 70) may need to either further refine, expand, or better deploy their people practices to create a more harmonious testing environ-

ment. Organizations at the upper end of the point scale should continue doing what they are now doing, and make only minor adjustments to continually improve their people-related skill sets.

Conclusion 2: Criterion Assessment

Referring to the scores you calculated for each Assessment Category on the Worksheet, evaluate your aptitude for each on a scale of two to eight, using the corresponding interpretation provided below:

Score   *Interpretation*

2 to 5   This score indicates a criterion in which improvement is needed. You should select this criterion for your plan of action. The chapter associated with this criterion (provided in the far right column of the Summarization Worksheet) should be studied and used to improve your personal skills and/or your organization's environment as it relates to the people side of testing.

6 to 8   This score indicates that you and/or your organization have a reasonable approach in place for this people-related software testing criterion. With a score of six or seven you can use the information in the chapter cited on the Worksheet to fine-tune your approach. However, your time would be better spent improving the areas in which you scored five points or less.

The remainder of the book is your pathway to progress. Use it to better understand your testing challenges, and to develop a plan of action to improve those skills in which you and/or your organization have an indicated weakness.

CHAPTER THREE

CHALLENGE #10: GETTING TRAINED IN TESTING

OVERVIEW

A commonly held belief about testing is that anyone who can operate a system can perform testing. The truth is that testing is a professional discipline, requiring unique skills that are anything but intuitive. Without training, testers are ill-equipped to meet the rigors of testing, especially in technically difficult situations. The people-related challenge of this chapter is to secure adequate support for training.

Although testing training is available through a variety of sources, a commitment and investment to obtain training are always required of testers and management. In some organizations, this need is recognized and met. In other organizations, self-motivation is the only way to get the training required to build testing skills.

In this chapter, we look at ways to raise management's awareness of the training needs of testers. We also explain how to map out your personal skill-building goals and objectives, which may include certification as a software test engineer.

25

STATE OF THE PRACTICE

The project is two months away from completion and management realizes that testing should be performed. The only question is, who should perform testing? With everyone on the project already hopelessly involved with the daily battles at hand in building the system, who has time to perform testing?

The idea occurs to management that fresh, independent people would be a good way to test the project. After all, there are several people in the end-user area that could be pulled together for about four weeks. If the end-users need help, additional contract resources can always be secured at a fairly low hourly rate to pound the keyboards.

In fairly short order, the ad hoc test team is assembled and testing commences. As the deadline approaches, defects have been found and corrected. Everything looks pretty good to the test team. Then, the moment of truth arrives. The project that has cost the organization nearly one million dollars to complete is ready to be placed into production.

Day one of the new system arrives, complete with T-shirts and balloons. There is only one problem: After two hours, calls to the help desk start pouring in, reporting strange results. Before long, the system response time starts to slow down severely. Customers are irate because they can't get quick answers to their telephone inquiries. Finally, the inevitable happens—the proverbial plug is pulled. "Oops, let's hope we can restore the old system. . . ."

What Went Wrong in This Scenario?

This story illustrates a classic misunderstanding of the skills required in testing. In the project described, the testers had never tested software before and, furthermore, had never been trained to test. Although many mistakes were made in the organization of the testing effort, a major error was the assumption that anyone could perform testing and find critical defects.

Testers face a challenge in defining and executing test cases that cover even a fraction of the possible system functions. To understand the universe of tests that can be performed, a tester must be aware of the possible sources of defects. These sources of defects are not a deeply shrouded mystery, but they are part of a growing body of knowledge that trained testers possess.

Without adequate training in testing techniques, testers are left to their own devices. Some of their tests will find obvious defects but will miss the subtle defects that can cause system failure. Untrained testers often do not understand the features and functions of the software they are assigned to test.

Some companies start entry-level people in the testing area as a form of training and move them to the "more meaningful" jobs in software development after they learn how to use the system. In such situations, as with the scenario described above, support for training is not received by the testers because

- management is not aware of the value of testing
- organizations are not aware of training resources
- organizations see training as an extra expense that can be cut
- testers feel they are too busy to attend training sessions
- in-house trainers often lack testing expertise
- testing is perceived as something anyone should be able to perform

IMPACT ON TESTING

The testing effort can consume fifty percent or more of a project's total cost. At the same time, less than one percent of software professionals have been formally trained in testing techniques. This is a huge imbalance.

Without training, important test cases are overlooked, planning is either not completed or not performed at all, defect information is not tracked, and tests are performed several times needlessly. In effect, testing becomes a craft rather than a repeatable process.

Training can help a tester fulfill his project responsibility and understand the kinds of testing that developers, technical support, and end-users usually perform. See Table 3.1. The intersection points in the table list the skills required to support testing.

Skill Categories and Descriptions

Below, the testing skills listed in Table 3.1 are divided into two categories: essential and optional. The essential skills are critical for effective testing. The optional skills add efficiency and optimize the testing process.

Essential Testing Skills

Test Planning: Analyzing a project to determine the kinds of testing needed, the kinds of people needed, the scope of testing (including what should and should not be tested), the time available for testing activities, the initiation criteria for testing, the completion criteria, and the critical success factors of testing.

Test Tool Usage: Knowing which tools are most appropriate in a given testing situation, how to apply the tools to solve testing problems effectively, how to organize automated testing, and how to integrate test tools into an organization.

Test Execution: Performing various kinds of tests, such as unit testing, system testing, user acceptance testing, stress testing, and regression testing. This can also include how to determine which conditions to test and how to evaluate whether the system under test passes or fails. Test execution can often be dependent on your unique environment and project needs, although basic testing principles can be adapted to test most projects.

Defect Management: Understanding the nature of defects, how to report defects, how to track defects, and how to use the information gained from defects to improve the development and testing processes.

Optional Skills

Risk Analysis: Understanding the nature of risk, how to assess project and software risks, how to use the results of a risk assessment to prioritize and plan testing, and how to use risk analysis to prevent defects and project failure.

Test Measurement: Knowing what to measure during a test, how to use the measurements to reach meaningful conclusions, and how to use measurements to improve the testing and development processes.

Test Case Design: Understanding the sources of test cases, test coverage, how to develop and document test cases, and how to build and maintain test data.

Building a Test Environment: Knowing how to create a test environment based on the technical requirements, how to implement configuration control for the test environment, and how to maintain the test environment.

Knowing What Kinds of Testing Should Be Performed

Table 3.1 shows three attributes of system development commonly subject to testing: function, structure, and quality. Functional testing tests the software from a cause/effect perspective. For example, if a certain function key is pressed, is the result correct? Other examples could include adding a new customer, opening a window on a GUI application, or updating data.

Structural testing requires a knowledge of the software code or system internals. This kind of testing seeks to test the logic and interfaces of a system. Examples of this kind of test would be testing each branch of an IF statement in a software module, or performing a stress test to determine how many concurrent users the system can handle.

Table 3.1.
Testing Skills Needed.

Who Tests?	What Do They Test?	System Functionality	System Structure	System Quality
Developers		Test Planning, Test Tool Usage, Test Execution, Risk Analysis, Test Case Design, Building a Test Environment	Test Planning, Test Tool Usage, Test Execution, Test Case Design, Building a Test Environment	Test Planning, Test Tool Usage, Test Execution, Risk Analysis, Test Case Design, Building a Test Environment
Independent Testers		Test Planning, Test Tool Usage, Test Execution, Defect Management, Risk Analysis, Test Measurement, Test Case Design, Building a Test Environment	Test Planning, Test Tool Usage, Test Execution, Test Case Design, Test Measurement	Test Planning, Test Tool Usage, Test Execution, Defect Management, Risk Analysis, Test Measurement, Test Case Design, Building a Test Environment
Technical Support		Does not usually perform	Test Planning, Test Tool Usage, Test Execution, Test Case Design, Building a Test Environment	Test Planning, Test Tool Usage, Test Execution, Test Case Design, Building a Test Environment
End-Users		Test Planning, Test Tool Usage, Test Execution, Defect Management, Risk Analysis, Test Case Design	Does not usually perform	Test Planning, Test Tool Usage, Test Execution, Defect Management, Risk Analysis, Test Case Design

System quality testing tests the things that a system should *be* as opposed to what the system should *do* (functional tests). Examples of this kind of testing would be usability testing for ease of use, performance testing for system performance, and reliability testing.

A tester needs to know the kinds of testing that should be performed on a project. With all the different kinds of projects under way in organizations, how is a tester supposed to know—without training—the most effective test methods? For example,

- client/server systems have a different set of testing concerns than traditional systems
- graphical user interfaces require a different approach than procedural on-line software
- user acceptance testing uses a different method of testing than system testing

Table 3.1 shows the skills needed for each kind of test, depending on the role of the tester: developer, independent tester, technical support, or end-user. After determining the testing skills needed, you can use Table 3.2 to find the best kinds of training. Here, each of the testing skills listed in Table 3.1 is related to training sources, such as seminars, conferences, books, and more, and is rated by degree of fitness based on the following scale:

Good Fit [1]: The training addresses specific issues that testers might face. Specific questions can be asked of and answered by the resource.
Acceptable [2]: The topic is discussed, but not to the degree that would meet everyone's needs. Questions may or may not be answered.
Marginal [3]: Some useful information will be learned, but application will likely be lacking. Questions are not answered.

Table 3.2.
Types of Test Training Available.

Training Types \ Skill Types	Test Planning	Test Tool Usage	Test Execution	Defect Management	Risk Analysis	Test Measurement	Test Case Design	Building a Test Environment
Seminars	1	3	1	1	1	1	1	1
Conferences	1	2	1	1	2	1	1	1
Vendor courses	2	1	1	1	3	3	2	1
Books	2	3	2	3	2	1	1	3
Videos	2	3	2	2	2	2	2	3
Self-study courses	2	3	3	3	3	2	2	3
In-house developed courses	1	1	1	1	2	1	1	3

1 = Good Fit, 2 = Acceptable, 3 = Marginal

Books contain details and can be referenced, but the author is not available to answer questions. Seminars contain information at a detailed level, but this must be applied to a variety of environments. Fortunately, if you have a question, the instructor should be able to answer it. Conferences are great places to learn what others are doing and what testing experts advise. A conference is not intended to provide a classroom experience, so there is usually a lot of interaction with peers and experts to learn—at least on a superficial level—new testing techniques.

The skill types introduced in Tables 3.1 and 3.2 can be used to answer the what, who, when, and how questions of testing.

What to Test
(Skills Required: Test Planning, Test Case Design, Risk Analysis)

A common question that testers pose is "What do we test?" That is an understandable question in light of the billions of possible test conditions.

The quality and extent of the testing effort depends on how well testing identifies and mitigates risk, and how much of the software function and structure are tested (coverage). Tests that meet these criteria are not created by spur-of-the-moment inspiration—they must be planned in advance. To understand how to write a test plan requires training in testing fundamentals, much like developing a data model requires training in the science of data modeling.

Without training, the tester is working at minimal effectiveness because he or she is not aware of the wide range of possible sources of test cases. Except in the simplest of cases, it is impossible to test all of the possible combinations of software functions. However, it is possible to identify critical software functions and develop a set of test cases that cover those functions, provided the tester knows how and where to find those cases.

Who Should Perform Testing
(Skills Required: Test Planning)

In contrast to the story at the beginning of this chapter, everyone should have a part in testing a project: developers, independent testers, end-users, and management. The question is, in which ways do these people contribute value to the testing effort? Certain roles facilitate certain types of testing more effectively:

- Developers are best suited to perform code-based tests at the unit level.
- Developers and/or independent testers are best suited to perform unit testing.
- Combinations of people with a variety of talents are often needed to test at the system level.
- Users should own the user acceptance testing effort.

If people are not matched to the appropriate type of test, a testing effort will prove ineffective. When users are told to test software at a unit level, there is a waste of time and talent. Unit testing involves testing each and every edit and function. When users get bogged down in detail, they lose their most important contribution to the testing effort—the business perspective. Users should be most concerned with validating that the system will support the needs of the organization. Again, Table 3.1 shows which project roles are best suited for the different kinds of testing and which skills are needed for effective testing.

When Testing Should Be Performed
(Skills Required: Test Execution, Test Planning)

Another major mistake made in the testing example was waiting until the end of the project to test the system. A trained tester would know that testing starts at the beginning of the project, with verification of system deliverables such as requirements documents, and continues throughout the life span of the system. Training in test execution and planning provides knowledge about the proper time for each phase of testing during a project.

One of the best ways to visualize the phases of testing and when they should be performed is the "V" diagram (see Figure 3.1). The "V" diagram shows the order of development activities along with the corresponding order of testing activities. In the case of a major system development project, work starts at the upper left of the "V" with defining the business or organizational need. Requirements are developed and the system is designed and built. In rapid application development (RAD), these activities are usually performed in cycles. You will notice that the requirements step involves two major kinds of tests: verification (inspections, walkthroughs, and other reviews) and validation (system testing). This same idea is applied to each development step to find defects throughout the project.

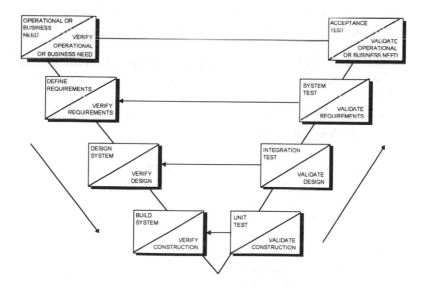

Figure 3.1: The "V" Diagram.

How to Test
(Skills Required: Test Execution, Defect Management, Test Measurement, Building a Test Environment)

A trained tester will know, among other things, how to write a test plan, how to create test cases, how to build an adequate test environment, how to perform a test, and how to evaluate the results of testing. These are the testing tasks that most people take for granted but that actually require a great deal of skill to perform. Without training, testers tend to reinvent the work of others through trial and error. The problem is that trial-and-error testing costs time and money that few projects can afford.

SOLUTIONS TO THE CHALLENGE

Of all the testing challenges, training is the easiest but not necessarily the least costly to address. As we discussed above, training can take the form of books, seminars, conferences, and even magazine articles and learn-at-lunch sessions (provided someone has the in-house testing expertise to teach them). The form of training you should obtain depends on

- the availability of the subject material in that format
- the degree of fitness for the skills needed (see Table 3.2)
- the amount of time budgeted for training
- the amount of money budgeted for training
- the level of in-house testing expertise

Raise Management Awareness of Testing

Without management support, the development of testing skills will be very slow, if they develop at all. The key is for management to understand how much time and money is wasted on trial-and-error testing. Management also needs to understand that expensive and high-risk systems are entrusted to testers to ensure that defects do not occur when used by end-users or customers. It's management's choice: Who would you rather have in this critical role, a trained and skilled tester or someone who is doing the best he can with the best ideas he can develop on his own?

Here are some steps you can take to raise management's awareness of testing and the need for skill-building:

1. *Calculate how much testing costs your organization.* Don't forget to include the cost of planning and reporting.
2. *Educate management in the cost of testing.* Show ways that the cost can be reduced through the use of more effective techniques. Most organizations can quickly reduce the cost of development and testing by at least ten percent by eliminating the waste and redundancy found in ad hoc testing processes.
3. *Explore other motivations for the benefits of testing.* For example, effective testing will help streamline your testing process and shorten the time to delivery.
4. *Build testing skill development into your personal goals and objectives.* Demonstrate to your management that you are committed to learning more about testing to add value to the organization. This means you might have to buy books on your own, but a little initiative goes a long way.
5. *Keep your eye out for articles about testing.* Route these articles to your management as you find them, to highlight the contribution skilled testers make on critical projects.
6. *Discuss your training needs with your management.* Explore ways together that you can find answers to your questions. If there is a relevant course available, discuss the possibility of attending and reporting the information back to the rest of the team.
7. *Find out if there is a training budget for your organization.* If there are funds available, it might be feasible to schedule an in-house training course for twenty or more people at a reasonable price.
8. *Be creative.* Buy another copy of this book, place a paper clip at this chapter, and leave it in your manager's in-basket as an anonymous gift!

Make Time for Training

The paradox of training is that when you need it the most, there isn't enough time. You'll want to put training into practice as soon as possible, but how do you make the time for training in the first place, when there is hardly time for testing? Here are some steps for getting the time for training:

1. *Build time for training into the project plan.* This makes training a planned event, not something extra to be squeezed in as time allows. Figure 3.2 shows a sample test plan that addresses training. Notice that the sample test plan is performed at a checkpoint. In a typical project, you would have a document like this for each project checkpoint, such as requirements definition, design, system testing, and so forth.
2. *Budget for training activities.* This will allow you to plan in advance which training you can secure.
3. *Match the training to your need.* To learn about many aspects of testing, you may require a week-long course. For a specific aspect of testing, a one-day course may suffice.

Develop Your Own Skills

As a tester, you have the ultimate responsibility for developing your skills. If your management supports your efforts in the form of paying for your training, that's great. If not, then you will need to find ways to develop skills that can fit into your personal budget. There are many tangible ways to develop your own testing skills:

1. *Make a list of your personal development goals.* These goals should include completion dates and what it will take on your part to achieve them.
2. *Build your own testing library.* Start with the books that address basic testing topics. A list of these are found in the Related Reading section at the back of this book.

PROJECT: OMNI	CHECKPOINT: System Testing
SCHEDULE/DATES	
Plans:	System test plans to be completed by September 30.
Training:	Training in testing techniques to start on September 7 and finish on September 14.
Testing Materials:	1 work room with a whiteboard, 4-drawer filing cabinet, and 2 telephones. Executable versions of the OMNI software.
Start Test:	October 15
Conclude Test:	November 15
BUDGET	
	$20,000
RESOURCES	
Equipment:	15 IBM-compatible 486 PCs attached to the local area network and 2 laser printers.
Software/ Documents:	Executable versions of the OMNI software, requirements documents for the OMNI system, OMNI system documentation and user guides.
Personnel:	3 developers from the OMNI project team, 1 quality assurance analyst, 3 representatives from each of the affected end-user departments, 1 internal auditor for testing the payroll subsystem.
TESTING MATERIALS	
System Documentation:	OMNI system requirements, data flow diagrams, entity-relationship diagrams, business process workflow diagrams, screen layouts, listing of all modules in the OMNI system.
Software to Be Tested:	All modules in the OMNI system, plus interfaces to the payroll and accounting systems.
Test Inputs:	Test cases as designed and documented by the test team.
Test Documentation:	Test scenarios, test scripts, and the system test plan. Defect reports from the system test.
Test Tools:	Capture/playback, defect tracking tool, test case generator.

Figure 3.2: System Checkpoint Administrative Worksheet (Part 1).

TEST TRAINING	
Type of Training:	Training in software and system testing techniques.
Personnel to Be Trained:	Project manager, QA analysts, end-users, internal auditor.
When:	September 7 to 14
Where:	Corporate training facility.
Training Staff/Vendor:	In-house testing course conducted by in-house training staff.
Training Materials:	Notebooks, overhead projector, VCR, and monitor.
TESTS TO BE CONDUCTED	
See attached list of test descriptions.	

Figure 3.2: System Checkpoint Administrative Worksheet (Part 2).

3. *Keep a clipping file.* This should include testing articles and other articles of interest that appear in computer trade magazines and other publications.
4. *Participate in local software quality organizations.* A listing of these groups appears in the back of this book.
5. *Continue the learning process.* As technologies change, so must your tool kit of techniques.

Certify Your Testing Skills

As you gain experience and training, you should apply to become a Certified Software Test Engineer (CSTE). This will add to your credibility and enhance your testing career. It tells your employer and others that you have developed the skills and obtained the experience to test software effectively. In addition, certification is something that you can carry to your next job to show evidence of demonstrated testing skills.

Your author Bill Perry's organization, the Quality Assurance Institute (QAI) of Orlando, Florida, has a certification program for people with two or more years of professional testing experience. Details on how to contact QAI are provided in the Resources section of this book.

SOLUTION IMPEDIMENTS

If you really want to build your skills in testing, no one can keep you from learning and refining them. Along the road of learning, you will likely face impediments that will require creative solutions. Many of these present themselves as "what if" or "how do I" questions, as we'll see throughout this book.

What if my management will not support my training needs?

Even if your current management does not support your training needs, there is hope. Things change and your situation a year from now can be greatly different from what it is today— that is why it is so important not to wait for management to start your skill-building process. Buy or check out the books you need to read, network with testers in other companies, and generally do what it takes to learn on your own. If your current situation does not change, you might choose to take your skills to an employer who will recognize and reward your initiative.

What if I do not have enough money to attend a testing seminar or conference?

If you're on your own to get training, courses can get expensive. Take advantage of every opportunity to network with other testers, attend local presentations on testing by test tool vendors, and check out testing sources on the Internet. In addition, many local libraries have books on testing that can start you on the road to gaining testing knowledge.

What if I do not have enough time for training?

The urgent often takes the place of the important. Ask yourself this question: "If I really knew what I was doing, would it take as long?" Probably not. Sometimes you have to make time to do the truly important things. Training is an investment that pays big dividends in both efficiency and effectiveness.

GUIDELINES FOR SUCCESS

- **Set personal goals.**

  If you set personal goals, you will be in a three percent minority of successful people. Success seldom happens without planning.

- **Seek management's assistance in building your testing skills, but don't wait for it.**

  Enlightened managers invest in people and reap dividends in prevented problems. Unenlightened managers focus on cutting costs, do not provide the tools to do the job right, and will instead spend much time and money on fixing problems.

- **Invest in yourself.**

  "What you become directly influences what you get"
  —Jim Rohn

- **Strive to add value to the testing effort.**

  Job security in America is a thing of the past. Companies are looking for the people who add value. This is the case whether you work for yourself or for someone else. A trained tester adds value to a project by knowing and applying sound testing methods. Effective testing methods can help eliminate waste and redundancy while increasing the number of defects found.

PLAN OF ACTION

While we have addressed solutions and impediments, let's look at an overall plan of action that ties everything together into your master approach for building testing skills.

1. Get management on your side by showing them

   - how much money is being spent on testing
   - the critical nature of software quality to your organization—that is, what could happen if a defect is found by users or customers
   - how much time and money could be saved by applying effective testing methods
   - the value that you personally could bring to the organization as a result of increasing your skill
   - initiative by starting to build your own skills

2. Develop your own skill-building goals and objectives by

- making a list of what you need to learn to be effective
- identifying resources for training and skill-building in testing
- planning to spend the time and money it takes to meet your skill-development goals
- staying on the lookout for training opportunities that you can easily participate in, such as local special interest groups, vendor test tool presentations, and the like
- getting certified as a Certified Software Test Engineer

3. Never stop learning!

CHAPTER FOUR

CHALLENGE #9: BUILDING RELATIONSHIPS WITH DEVELOPERS

OVERVIEW

When testing is viewed as something that someone else does, two sides are automatically created. Yet, everyone in an organization should be involved in testing, because testing is a shared responsibility.

Testing is also an *interdependent* activity. Each group performs its tasks, but is dependent on others for its success. The term *independent testing* implies to some that testers should work in isolation from developers. This often leads to developers blaming testers for delays—and testers blaming developers for defects. The challenge is to move from the us-versus-them mindset to the interdependent teamwork approach.

STATE OF THE PRACTICE

Randy Rice relates his experience: It was my first day on the job as the newly hired test team leader for a large, mission-critical project. The company had experienced a recent failure in a previous attempt at building the same system, so there was already a dark cloud hanging over the project.

One of my first meetings was with the CEO of the company. He was gracious and kind in welcoming me to work for the company. As he explained his optimism about the current system effort, he made it very clear that the company's future rested on the successful implementation of the new system project.

The CEO's charge to me that day was one that I will never forget. He said, "I want you to test the heck out of that system. Tear it up if you have to, because it has to be right." Being the young and obedient new employee I was, I said, "Yes sir, you can count on me." This conversation set the tone for the test in my mind. I was the bulldog and the project team was the steak.

I planned the test, recruited the test team, and on the first day of the test we did what many testers do—we sat around waiting for the system to be available for testing. It didn't take long for the team to find a fair amount of defects. As the defects mounted, so did the tensions between the developers and the test team.

The source of the tension was not due to finding defects, but the attitude we had toward the developers. It wasn't that we disliked each other, it was that we were approaching the test from an adversarial attitude, thinking that would result in a more rigorous test. I remember even watching the movie *Patton* to get psyched up for testing.

Soon, we reached a point where no one would go to lunch with us, so we called for a truce. After that, the testing was not relaxed or compromised, but we operated with a different attitude—one of cooperation.

Instead of seeing the development group as "the other side," we realized that both testers and developers were team members who shared the goal of seeing a successful system implementation. To ease tension, we added a person from the development group to the test team. The result was a much smoother relationship with the developers that enabled us to test more effectively. Sure, we had problems and the project looked bleak at times, but the system was eventually implemented successfully and everyone lived to talk about it.

We had discovered a built-in conflict in testing that must be understood. On one hand, testers are supposed to find defects and be destructive in testing to the point that the system is exercised in extreme conditions (sometimes, conditions that everyone else on the project swears will never happen). On the other hand, testers need to work in cooperation with developers to resolve defects, to understand the system, and to keep testing on track. The challenge is to attain the right balance of rigorous testing and cooperation in order to function as an effective team.

IMPACT ON TESTING

An adversarial attitude adds negative tension to a project and detracts from the drive toward successful completion. Of course, the testers need to focus on finding defects, but there are ways to find defects without alienating the rest of the project team.

Figure 4.1 compares a traditional testing organization with one that applies a teamwork approach. The key difference is that testing responsibilities are shared. Everyone is responsible for a quality product and nobody wins when a defect goes undetected. Furthermore, people are not relying on someone else to find the defects.

An adversarial relationship has more negative impact on testers and developers than on testing. While testing can proceed, negative attitudes eat away at the very inner being of both testers and developers. The incidents that occur during the day usually are taken home with people at night and also impact their families. Seeing the other side as the enemy can result in

- low morale
- slow or stalled projects
- inefficient testing

- poor physical and mental health
- destroyed relationships
- termination of employment
- project failure

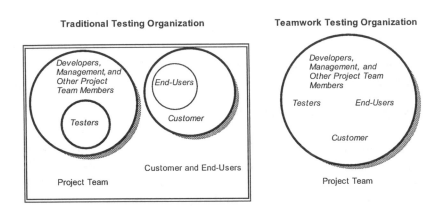

Figure 4.1: Traditional Testing Organization Contrasted to Teamwork Testing Organization.

Adversarial testing does not add to the rigor of testing, but does add to the overall stress level of the project. The us-versus-them attitude has a negative impact on two major areas: testing progress and group morale. We discuss these in greater detail below.

The Impact on Testing Progress

The negative impact on testing comes from delays and bottlenecks caused by

- the lack of communication between developers and testers
- the lack of cooperation between developers and testers in solving problems and resolving defects

Lack of Communication

Poor communication is a major cause of project failure, and blocked lines of communication are absolutely detrimental to testing. A good way to gauge the quality of communication is to study defect or incident reports. Poor communication is manifested by statements such as, "It's broken. FIX IT!" The reply is sometimes just as terse: "If you would use the system as designed, IT WOULD WORK!"

Open communication is essential to keeping the testing effort on track. Status reports, for example, let everyone on the project team know what is going on. Too often, an entire test database is deleted—after days of work are spent on it—because the database analyst doesn't know anyone is using it.

Lack of Cooperation

Cooperation is needed on such simple tasks as getting a computer operator to run a special job, or on tougher tasks, such as getting people to spend several hours or a weekend on a certain effort. Most often, testers need cooperation from developers to track the work in progress. To developers, filling out forms and other documentation may seem like jumping through hoops, but the information they provide is essential for management of the test environment.

The Impact on Group Morale

Teams get along, but groups do not necessarily work well together. That's why it may be incorrect to call a group a *team*. When a project ceases to be a team effort, then morale is often low, sides are taken, loyalties are divided, and turf is staked out. It's anything but a joy to be part of such a group.

Taking Sides

In organizations that have a negative culture, the end-users are usually alienated from developers, management is alienated from employees, and the business may even be alienated from its customers. Sadly, the management in these organizations may think it is good for testers to be totally separate from the people developing the software, even to the point of being seen as the bad guys. The reality is that this kind of independence is much less productive than interdependence. To make progress in testing, testers and developers must recognize that they are dependent on each other.

Divided Loyalties

Whenever you fall on one side of an issue, there will come a time when you must defend your side or adjust your position. This is one of the big reasons the people-oriented Tester 2 mentioned in Chapter 1 can become very unhappy and stressed out. As a tester, you might have a good friend who is a developer trying very hard to get a software application into production. After testing the software and finding defects, you may find yourself in the uncomfortable position of turning the application back to your friend with a defect report instead of a clean test report. A divided loyalty can develop in a situation such as this, when you would like to see your friend succeed but you have to perform a thorough test. In an atmosphere of cooperation, this situation can be managed, but in an us-versus-them environment, this may end a friendship.

Staking Out Turf

When you operate by taking sides, it is only natural to stake out territory in which you feel safe. Humans have been doing this throughout history. One of the most obvious signs of a territorial attitude is a resistance to independent assessments, inspections, audits, or testing—even in the presence of high defect rates. Sometimes, the turf battle is ultimately lost with the dissolution of a testing organization. That is why management support for testing is essential.

SOLUTIONS TO THE CHALLENGE

Adversarial testing can be difficult to change because it often has roots in the culture of an organization. While other issues can be addressed in the short term, cultural issues may take months or years to resolve. Transforming adversarial organizations is the Holy Grail of management.

The primary solution is to view testing as a win-win activity that involves many people throughout a project's life cycle. Teamwork is essential, as is seeing the other side's perspective. All other efforts, such as improving communication, developing a spirit of cooperation, and improving morale, are based on teamwork.

Adopt a Win-Win Approach

The win-win position described by Stephen Covey in *The 7 Habits of Highly Effective People* applies well to testing. On one hand, testers are looking for defects, and in effect, each defect found is a win for the testers. On the other hand, developers want to successfully implement the system. Getting the project into production is a win for the developers.

When testers find defects and use this information negatively against developers, the testers win and the developers lose respect, credibility, and a sense of accomplishment. When developers override the recommendations of testers and implement a system with defects, the developers win, but the testers lose when they get blamed for the defects found in production.

A win-win is achieved when everyone on the project understands that a defect discovered and resolved is one step closer to a quality system. The sooner the defects are found and fixed, the better. The more people looking for defects, the better. When a defective system is implemented, everyone loses, including the customer or end-user.

Widen Your View of Testing

Effective testing throughout the project's life cycle depends on the involvement of many people, not just a separate group toward the end of a project.

Involving people from all areas of a project results in interdependence instead of independence. Everyone shares a stake in the positive outcome of the project. Interdependence emphasizes that people acting alone cannot make the project succeed.

When people understand they need help from others to succeed, communication improves. Information that might have been kept secret before is shared because it is needed to solve problems. It no longer matters who looks the best.

Move from "Us versus Them" to "Us and Them"

Now that we've seen specific benefits in changing basic behavior patterns, let's ask the question, "Is it possible to move from an attitude of adversity to one of teamwork?" Yes, it is possible, but not necessarily easy.

There are success stories of people who have made the transition from an adversarial to a teamwork approach. The common thread is working from the inside out. The best leaders are those who have internalized the win-win approach. It takes an inner awakening and time for this transformation to happen. Slogans, buttons, and posters will not effect inner transformation. Understanding who you are and seeing the vision of what needs to be accomplished will start the transformation process. To understand yourself, it takes reflection and knowing your own personal mission. What are you trying to do in your life? in your company? in your family?

Once you fully realize that your success depends on others, you can start building the bridges that affect teamwork. Although this transformation does not have a formula (if it did we would be rich), there are several principles that can guide you to an us-*and*-them approach.

1. *Organize testing to involve people from all aspects of the project.* Testing should be a process, not a craft or art. The process determines who performs testing and when it is performed. A good testing process will start on the first day of the project, involve people from all areas, and will continue until the specified quality criteria are met.
2. *Focus on the product, not the producer.* When the focus is on the producer, blame is assigned either consciously or unconsciously. Focusing on the product keeps blame out of the picture and keeps the lines of communication open.
3. *Pay attention to the cultural issues.* Not everyone will be on board with the testing agenda. Keep emphasizing the value realized for the effort involved.
4. *Secure and maintain management support.* When management conveys by their words and actions that testing is important, your chances of success increase.

SOLUTION IMPEDIMENTS

How do we get everyone on the project involved in testing?

Testing should be process driven. Likewise, the testing organization should be shaped by the needs of the process. In this regard, testing should be seen as an important part of the overall project and built into the project plan and staffing estimates.

In addition to testers, developers and end-users should also be on the test team. They bring a useful combination of talents and knowledge to the testing effort. Some organizations have testing "intern" programs where developers and end-users spend a limited amount of time on the test team, then return to their regular duties.

What if people don't want to be involved in testing?

Let's face it, testing is not a glamorous job. Some people do not see the value of testing. To them, testing is like documentation—no one likes to do it, but it really needs to be done. With this view, testing will at best be tolerated and at worst be ignored.

To get people on board with the concept of testing, you must first emphasize the importance of testing and how it relates to the end result of delivering quality software or a quality system. You will need to start marketing the importance of testing to management, developers, customers, and end-users. How do you show the value of testing to those who might not even care to know in the first place? One of the best ways is to focus on WIIFM (What's in it for me?). In this case, you need to show what's in it for them.

Realize that people are motivated by different things. A manager might be motivated by a lower cost of finding and fixing defects. A developer might be motivated by fewer night calls or not coming in on the weekend to fix a problem.

How do we criticize constructively?

One of the surest ways to alienate people in the testing effort is to be critical of the producer instead of the product. In some organizations, this is a cultural pattern. How can you break the pattern?

First, you have to put yourself in the producer's role. You can do this by going through a review of your own work by someone else. If you really want to feel how a developer feels during a test, let some developers review one of your deliverables, such as a test plan or other document. Even when care is taken to avoid negative comments, it is often an uncomfortable experience for the producer.

Listen for the tone of comments and words such as, "You should have . . ." or "Why did you . . . ?" The key word in these examples is "you." Less critical phrases are, "What are some other options?" or "What is the purpose of this section?"

Changing critical patterns is not easy because we are so used to focusing on the person rather than on the product. With practice and attention to the words we speak, it is possible over time to create a less critical atmosphere.

How do I get management support for testing?

Testing is quality control. Without testing, defects will be found by the customers or end-users. Most management will want to ensure that acceptable levels of quality are delivered, but will keep a close eye on the budget.

Risk analysis is another way to raise management's support of testing. Management should be fully aware of the risks involved should a critical defect be found by a customer. Some defects may have little consequence, while others could have catastrophic results. The degree of testing should be in proportion to the risks.

The point to remember is that when the role of testing is not understood and the testing organization is weak and ineffective, management is not getting the best return on investment. "Us versus them" is an ineffective way to test and results in spending more time and money than necessary.

GUIDELINES FOR SUCCESS

- **Build the test team so that participants from a variety of disciplines are involved.**

  It is hard to be "us versus them" when "them is us"!

- **Make win-win the only way you operate.**

  "We have committed the golden rule to memory; let us now commit it to life."
  —Edwin Markham

- **Keep the lines of communication open.**

  "The way we communicate with others and with ourselves ultimately determines the quality of our lives."
  —Anthony Robbins

- **Keep working on yourself.**

  "If you work only on the problem at hand, you will get by for today. If you work on yourself, you will excel for a lifetime."
  —Jim Rohn

PLAN OF ACTION

1. Work on yourself first. Examine your own attitudes toward others. Put yourself in the producer's shoes and feel how criticism causes negative feelings.

2. Study other works on human interaction and potential. One of the best is *The 7 Habits of Highly Effective People* by Stephen Covey.

3. Keep a personal journal. Keep track of and study what works and what doesn't.

4. Make a conscious effort to show others in the organization the value of testing and what it can mean to them. Focus on the benefits and describe a clear picture of the envisioned results.

5. Involve others in the testing effort. Build a test team comprised of testers, developers, and users that test throughout the project. This matches the right person to a particular testing task and spreads the testing responsibility.

CHAPTER FIVE

CHALLENGE #8: TESTING WITHOUT TOOLS

OVERVIEW

One reason that testing is often overlooked or ignored is that it takes so much time and can be tedious work. Yet, testing is extremely important: A small error in performing a test can let a defect pass directly to the customer or end-user. One common approach is to hire more testers. The only problem is that humans make mistakes and do not always have the endurance or the patience to effectively perform the huge numbers of tests required for most projects.

The logical solution is to use the right tools for the job, combined with the right process and properly trained people. However, tools cost money and the funding must come from management. In many organizations, management expects testers to compensate for the expense of a test tool with manual testing, even if it means overtime and burnout. The question is, How do you persuade management to purchase the tools you need?

Another question that must be answered is, How do we make test tools part of the testing process once we buy them? Most people know that tools alone have never solved a problem; tools must be worked into the process. This chapter explains the ins and outs of test tools. We discuss what happens when you don't have the right test tools, how to lay the groundwork for buying a test tool, how to select a test tool, and how to make the test tool effective in your organization.

STATE OF THE PRACTICE

The project is behind schedule and the independent test team of three people is working twelve hours a day under contract to test the work of twenty people. Several months ago, the need for an automated test tool was recognized and a tool was selected, but the purchase decision was never made because other needs were of higher priority to the management team. As a result, the testers must execute manual scripts every time a program is revised and resubmitted for testing.

As a critical deadline approaches, the test team must not only work excessive hours to keep up with the developers, but they must find any new defects that are introduced as a result of fixing a defect. Due to the fatigue of working twelve-hour days, weeks on end, combined with the monotony of testing the same program over and over, more defects are missed in testing. In effect, the testing effort is in a downward spiral—the harder the test team works, the worse things get.

The problem doesn't last long, however. Because of excessive defects, the customer does not accept delivery of the software and refuses to pay for it. This causes a major cash flow problem on the project. After a few days, the contracting company is facing bankruptcy and everyone on the project is looking for work.

Did the project fail for lack of a test tool? No, but an automated test tool, combined with an effective testing process, would have reduced the time required to test basic functions and would have allowed the testers to focus on critical tests.

Many of the defects would have been caught before they went to the customer.

In this scenario, there was simply too much work for the test team to handle. With a restricted cash flow, there was not enough money to hire more testers and it was too late to buy a test tool. Had the purchase of an automated test tool been regarded as important as a database management tool, a lot of time and money could have been saved by automating repetitive tasks.

IMPACT ON TESTING

The lack of test tools can have a major impact on testing. One of the unique characteristics of testing is that testers do the same thing over and over, that is, they execute test cases. It is possible to have billions of possible test cases, yet testers only have time to perform a small fraction of these. In addition, tests must be rerun if defects are found and changes are made. Capture/playback and script execution tools offer the greatest benefit in regression and stress/performance testing. Other tools, like test case generators and test data generators, can benefit many kinds of testing. Below, we discuss the selection and use of test tools, starting with the reasons for automated testing.

- **Manual testing is imprecise and unreliable.**

  At best, manual testing involves following a test script and executing test cases. At worst, manual testing is random and there is no way to repeat a test. In the best case of following a written script, it is up to the tester's skills and abilities to follow the script exactly, observe every aspect of the software's performance, and document the test results completely. In manual testing, there is always a degree of doubt that the test was performed exactly as planned. In addition, there is no way to reproduce the test to verify the exact actions performed. True regression testing requires that a previous test be repeated exactly and compared to the previous results. Any degree of error can invalidate the test, resulting in defects going undetected.

- **Manual testing is boring.**

The boredom of testing is one reason defects slip past testers. When tests must be performed repeatedly, automated tools not only remove the tedium of testing, but can identify minute differences from previous tests. These differences can indicate the presence of a defect.

- **Manual testing is labor intensive.**

During a typical testing effort, there is not enough time in the schedule to perform a minimal amount of testing, not to mention the repeated testing that is required in regression testing. A test that takes an hour to perform manually can be performed in a minute or less with an automated test tool. Multiply this time difference by hundreds of tests and you can see the impact on the testing work load.

The impact of increased testing speed can be seen especially during rapid application development (RAD). With RAD, a new version of the software can be generated daily. If the tests take four weeks to perform, test coverage will decrease, even as the target release is missed and exceeded (see Figure 5.1). Automated test tools help testers keep up with RAD by compressing the testing time, as shown in Figure 5.2. We discuss these figures further in Chapter 8.

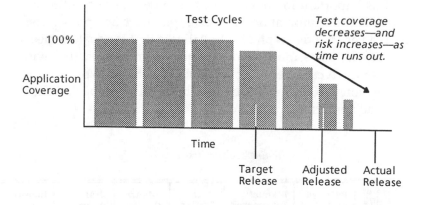

Figure 5.1: Manual Testing (courtesy of Rational Software).

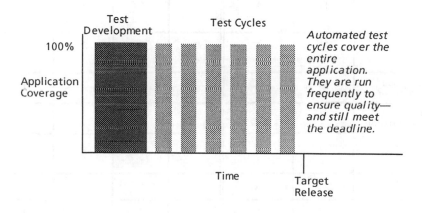

Figure 5.2: Automated Testing (courtesy of Rational Software).

Table 5.1 rates the impact of test tools on the phases of testing. Some of the test tools shown are manual; others are automated. Some tools are better suited to a particular test phase than others. The relative cost is defined as high (H), moderate (M), or low (L). Manual test usage is indicated by "M," and automated

61

test usage is indicated by "A." The degree of fitness is scored as a good fit (1), limited use (2), or not recommended (3).

It is important to understand that some types of testing are not suited for automation. For example, user acceptance testing is a very hands-on phase. To validate that the system meets user needs, users must spend adequate time interacting with the system. A capture/playback tool can be used to record user test sessions, to document the test, but script playback defeats the hands-on testing objective.

Table 5.1.
Testing Tools by Test Phase.

Phase of Testing Test Tool Categories	Relative Cost	Manual/ Automated	Unit Testing	Integra- tion/ System Testing	User Accep- tance Testing	Regres- sion Testing
Capture/ Playback	H	A	1	1	2	1
Automated Test Execution	H	A	1	1	3	1
Test Coverage Analyzer	M	A	1	2	3	2
Test Case Generator	M	A	1	1	2	1
Test Data Generator	M	A	1	1	1	1
Logic and Complexity Analyzer	H	A	1	2	3	3
Defect Tracker	L-M	A	1	1	1	1
Test Manager	M	A	1	1	1	1
Checklist	L	M	1	1	1	1
Flowchart	L	M	1	1	1	3
Test Script	M-H	A, M	1	1	1	1

Following are descriptions of the test tool categories cited in Table 5.1.

Capture/Playback

Capture/playback tools allow a test session to be captured or written to a file in a format that can be played back at a later time. These tools also have the ability to compare one set of test results to a previous set of test results. That is why capture/playback tools are essential for true regression testing—they can compare tests without human error.

Many of the capture/playback tools allow the user to modify the test scripts or procedures to add loops and conditional logic. You can even modify the scripts to read and write data.

Benefits: Executes and compares tests faster and more accurately than manual testing; records exactly which actions were performed during a test; performs tests in an unattended mode and documents results. These tools have their greatest benefit in regression and performance testing.

Automated Test Execution

Not every automated testing tool uses a capture method to create test scripts or procedures. Some tools use test scripts coded by testers. These tools also offer test comparison capabilities. Except for the script capture aspect, these are very similar to capture/playback tools.

Benefits: Executes and compares tests faster and more accurately than manual testing; performs tests in an unattended mode and then documents results. As with capture/playback tools, these tools have their greatest benefit in regression and performance testing.

Test Coverage Analyzer

Test coverage analyzers indicate the degree a module or system was exercised during a test. Test coverage may be expressed in lines of code tested, decisions tested, paths tested, or system paths tested, among others.

Benefits: Identifies areas of the system or the software that have not been tested; measures the degree of test completion.

Test Case Generator

Test case generators are intelligent tools that accept input from software requirements, data models, object models, and other system deliverables. This input is analyzed and translated into test cases that exercise the system with a minimal amount of redundancy.

Benefits: Saves time by automatically generating test cases that could take days or weeks to build manually; eliminates redundancy by building test cases that achieve the most test coverage with the minimum number of test conditions.

Test Data Generator

Test data generators are used to populate test files and databases without regard to the combinations of data. The test data are often random, but can be used to supplement test data created from specific test cases.

Benefits: Saves time by populating test files that would normally be populated through manual data entry.

Logic and Complexity Analyzer

Logic and complexity analyzers are used to measure the complexity of a software module or system. This is useful information since complexity can be a contributor to software defects. These tools can also present a graphical display of the logical paths in a software module or system.

Benefits: Identifies complex logic for risk analysis and determines software maintainability; maps complex logic for complete test coverage of a software module or section of code.

Defect Tracker

Defect trackers allow defect information to be collected and routed to the proper person(s) for resolution. Most defect trackers can be installed on a Local Area Network, and the defect information can be treated like e-mail. Defect trackers allow the user to create summary reports and to graph defect trends.

Benefits: Garners valuable information to be studied for defect trends; creates paperless defect reports that are not easily lost or misplaced; obtains, summarizes, and reports defect status quickly and easily.

Test Manager

Test management tools help organize and track test products, such as test scripts, test cases, and test progress.

Benefits: Improves controllability and management of testing; determines test status more easily. These tools can help drive the continuous improvement process by identifying the sources of defects.

Checklist

Checklists prompt the tester for things to include during a test or test-related activity.

Benefits: Adds completeness and consistency to testing at a low cost.

Flowchart

Flowcharts show a logical order of events to be followed when performing a process.

Benefits: Documents processes to be tested, making it possible to identify all logical paths through the process and to achieve complete test coverage.

Test Script

Test scripts show the sequential order of events to be performed during a test session. Test scripts can be manual or automated.

Benefits: Can be performed by someone unfamiliar with the process to be tested; allows the test to be repeated.

If you would like more information about these or other categories of test tools, refer to your author Bill Perry's book *Effective Methods of Systems Testing.*

SOLUTIONS TO THE CHALLENGE

Educate Management on the Use of Test Tools

As with so many other testing issues, you must have support from your management or you will be limited in your success. If you understand the key motivations for management, you will focus on the monetary and time-to-delivery benefits of using test tools. There are three phases of gaining support for any kind of technology, and these apply especially for acquiring and implementing test tools:

1. *Raise awareness.* You must make sure your management is aware of the kinds of test tools available. Articles are frequently published in the trade press about test tools, and many are written from the standpoint of how an organization solved a testing problem. Keep an eye out for these kinds of articles and route them to your management. You can also route brochures and other tool vendor advertisements to your management to raise awareness.
2. *Increase understanding.* After management is aware of the kinds of test tools available and how these tools can benefit your projects, you can start the education process. In this phase, you are concerned with learning about the distinctions between tools. For example, you might explore the differences between the capture/playback and automated test execution approaches to test automation. You need to understand the issues surrounding each tool and how the tool fits into your environment.

   There are a variety of ways to increase the understanding of test tools. Some tool vendors offer "road shows," or live, full-day or half-day demos of their tools in a public setting. Consider scheduling time with your manager to attend one of these sessions in your area. If this is not possible, many vendors will send you a complete set of materials including demo diskettes. Many diskette-based demos can be viewed in thirty minutes or less.

3. *Set expectations.* This might be the most important thing you do. Unrealistic expectations in any area can set the stage for major disappointment down the road. Make sure that management is aware that the tools are only as effective as the people that use them.

Many organizations have tools, but often the tools are largely ignored. At some time in the past, someone put time, effort, and money into bringing these tools into the organization, but something happened, or didn't happen, that kept people from applying the tools to their daily work.

Management needs to understand that a tool alone is not the answer to the problem. Most managers know this intellectually, but emotionally keep believing that the tool is the solution. Actually, tools are a part of the solution. The other parts of the solution are people and processes (see Figure 5.3).

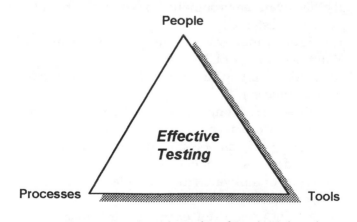

Figure 5.3: The Relationship of People, Tools, and Processes for Effective Testing.

Perform a Tool Survey

Before rushing to performing a tool search, take an inventory of the tools your organization currently owns. In large organizations, it is common for many tools to be owned—but often few people are aware of them.

A good place to start in performing a tool inventory is with your system administrator. You can also conduct a test tool survey to see which tools people are currently using and which tools would be of most help. Keep track of the responses and the people who provide input to the survey. A tool search should be a team effort, so stay on the lookout for potential team members.

Define Your Requirements

Shopping for a test tool is like shopping for anything else. If you don't know what you want or need before you start, you will probably buy the wrong thing.

Defining the tool requirements should be a team activity, since each group that will use the tool will have unique needs. The scope of tool requirements should include

- the hardware environment (for example, mainframe, PC, or workstation)
- the operational environment (for example, MVS, Windows, OS/2, or UNIX)
- the kinds of testing supported (for example, regression or performance)
- the phases of testing (for example, unit, integration, system, or acceptance)
- the people performing testing (for example, developers, independent testers, or end-users)
- the types of software (for example, character-based, GUI, or object-oriented)
- the type of project (for example, traditional waterfall approach, rapid application development, or prototyping)

- the budget
- the vendor training availability
- the vendor technical support availability

Perform a Cost/Benefit Analysis

At some point in the test tool proposal process, you will need to document the costs and benefits of the test tools you want to acquire. Many vendors have examples of successful cost/benefit studies they will share with you. In performing cost/benefit studies, don't forget to consider how the tools can

- benefit each phase of testing
- involve multiple groups in using the tools: users, developers, testers, and others
- reduce rework due to defects
- prevent defects
- streamline the testing process
- document tests
- isolate and reproduce defects for correction
- measure your test effectiveness
- control, manage, and predict the testing effort
- reduce the time-to-delivery
- reduce the number of test cases performed while increasing test coverage
- cross-reference a test to a specific requirement

Investigate Tools Available

One of the best places to start a tool search is on the Web. The testing tool market is changing at such a rapid pace, with mergers, acquisitions, and new products and vendors, it takes an interactive medium to keep up with it all. A search using the string, "software testing" +tools, on one or more of the major Internet search engines, should get you plenty of initial hits. Then you should be able to narrow your list to about three to five tools that are a good fit for your requirements. It is better to start contacting vendors after arriving at the short list to reduce the amount of personal communication required to deal with the tool vendors.

Integrate Test Tools with an Effective Testing Process

To quote Watts Humphrey on this point,

> Automation might make an effective software process more effective, but a chaotic one even worse—often at considerable expense. Many managers who are not familiar with software issues thus emphasize tools and ignore the critical need for better management and technical methods. Tools are important—unquestionably so—but they should not distract us from the greater need for appropriate process management methods.[1]

SOLUTION IMPEDIMENTS

What if my management does not see the need for test tools?

You have an educational process ahead of you. However, take heart in how the adoption of technology has progressed in recent years. In 1982, companies were reluctant to buy one personal computer for an entire department. Now, PCs are standard office equipment. Keep focusing on how test tools can help reduce the cost of testing and shorten the time-to-delivery—two messages that really speak to managers.

What if I can't get funding for test tools?

Do the best you can with the tools at hand while measuring the cost of testing. Once you know how much testing costs the organization, you can make an informed cost/benefit proposal for a test tool. If funding is still withheld, do the best you can with what you've got. Remember that humans can only do so much. You may be tempted to compensate for the lack of tools

---

[1] Watts Humphrey, "Software and the Factory Paradigm," *Software Engineering Productivity Handbook,* ed. Jessica Keyes (New York: McGraw-Hill, 1992), p. 322. Reproduced with permission of The McGraw-Hill Companies.

with your own physical ability, by working until midnight every night for several weeks, for example. Don't let this happen to you! If management will not provide the money for tools, they should expect less testing, slower testing, and inefficient testing.

What if no tools exist for my environment?

This is where you have to get creative. Many of the tools on the market today were created by someone to fill a need in a particular environment. You might have to develop your own tool, if possible. You can also check with other organizations in similar environments to see which tools they use. Testing conferences are a good place for this kind of networking.

What if other people in the organization do not want to use test tools?

This is why tools need to be part of a process, not just something that can be used as the need arises. For example, a certain level of code coverage in unit testing may be set as a test standard. By using a test coverage tool and a unit testing process that incorporates rigorous structural testing, you will be able to measure your success in meeting the standard.

With any tool or process, acceptance is essential for success. Our suggestion is that the tools and processes should be "owned" by the people using them. By ownership, we mean that the team selects the tools and the processes to be used in testing.

GUIDELINES FOR SUCCESS

- **Secure management support for acquiring test tools.**

  As in other efforts, your success in acquiring test tools will depend on the cooperation of others, primarily management. Management support will be needed for funding and to show the importance of using test tools to people who will be using them. If people don't see management support, they will see the effort as unimportant.

- **Use a team approach when selecting a tool.**

  "Plans fail for lack of counsel, but with many advisers they succeed."
  —Proverbs 15:22

- **Make good use of what you have.**

  It doesn't make sense to keep adding tools if you already have adequate test tools in place. The only way to determine if you need test tools is to perform a tool inventory. Many times, little is known about a tool after its champion leaves the organization.

- **Maximize tool use with people and processes.**

  A test tool without an effective process and trained people will only let you perform a bad test faster.

  "You can cut down a tree with a hammer, but it takes about 30 days. If you trade the hammer for an ax, you can cut it down in about 30 minutes. The difference between 30 days and 30 minutes is skill."
  —Jim Rohn

- **Use the right tools.**

  To extend the quotation of Jim Rohn cited above: You can cut down a tree with an ax in about thirty minutes. If you use a chain saw, you can cut it down in about thirty seconds. The difference between thirty minutes and thirty seconds is *more power*.

- **Make tool usage mandatory.**

  If you are really serious about making tool usage a reality in your organization, it must be a mandatory part of the process. Otherwise, the message is, "It's all right to use tools or not to use tools. Do whatever you think is best." This is like saying, "Okay, this team can build software with visual tools, and the rest of you who like COBOL, just keep writing code manually." The result is a nonstandard software development process and a slow adoption process of development tools. The same logic also applies to test tool adoption.

PLAN OF ACTION

1. Identify the stakeholders. These are people who can help you succeed or people who can prevent you from succeeding. Management should be among the stakeholders.

2. Lay the groundwork by raising test tool awareness among the stakeholders.

3. Identify or build the testing process. If a testing process is needed, a team should be formed to define and deploy the process.

4. Get approval and initiate a project to build a test toolbox. The test toolbox will include all the tools needed to perform testing effectively and to support the testing process. You might choose to build the test toolbox in phases, based on priority and criticality.

5. Form a team to identify which tools are already in place and to specify which tools are needed.

6. Use the tool selection team to identify the tool requirements. If multiple tools are needed, the team can prioritize the needs.

7. Identify the selection criteria. These will define how the tools will be judged.

8. Perform a tool search using all available information sources and tool directories.

9. Contact the qualified tool vendors for detailed information.

10. Evaluate the finalists.

11. Select the tool.

12. Develop the implementation plan, including integration of the tool and the testing process.

13. Train the staff in the new process and in how to use the tool to support the process.

14. Continue improving the process.

15. Continue training people as they are hired and as refresher training is needed.

CHAPTER SIX

CHALLENGE #7: EXPLAINING TESTING TO MANAGERS

OVERVIEW

With all of the other system activities competing for management's attention, testing has never traditionally ranked high on management's list of interests or priorities. To some, testing is seen as a trivial activity that is performed at the end of a project "just to make sure everything works," as if there is no doubt that the system will work as expected from day one. To others, testing is an intimidating task that only experts can understand.

The truth is that testing should be an integral part of building and deploying information systems. Testing does not need to be complex and difficult to be effective. Most people can be trained to be very good testers, whether they have a technical background or not. Testing is like any other system development activity in that it must be managed. Someone must be responsible for defining processes, selecting tools, facilitating test activities, and working with testers to resolve issues.

Without management's guidance and direction, testing becomes haphazard and ineffective.

In this chapter, we discuss the accurate view of testing and how to raise management's awareness of it. When management understands the risks of ineffective testing and what it takes to have effective testing, hopefully testing will move from a side function to the essential function of quality control. After all, any activity that consumes half of a project's time deserves more than just a little attention.

STATE OF THE PRACTICE

Joe, the test team leader, is not having a good day. He has just learned that the development schedule has slipped—again. The test team will not be able to start testing the software until two weeks into the planned six-week testing schedule. As Joe had feared, the final delivery deadline will remain the same.

In fact, his management has already committed to the customer that the software will be delivered on the promised date, regardless of the test results. The project team's mission during testing has become to find and fix as many defects as possible during the testing. The team's motto is "Focus on the big ones and let everything else slide."

Joe's request for more testers or a tool to help deal with the work load was denied by management. Management felt that the money would be better invested in a nicer package design for the software and a party for the project team. Joe gets the feeling that his job is a formality on the project. He feels that he and his team are only testing because of management's attitude that every project should be tested, at least a little.

That evening, Joe talks with Pat, a good friend who is a tester at a company across town. She sympathizes with Joe, having struggled with similar issues in the past. However, she's excited because the management at her company is trying innovative approaches to testing. Her management team is focusing more on the process than on the product. Everyone on the project team is involved in testing in Pat's company. One of the most significant changes is that if the project steering committee, including the leader of testing, does not unanimously agree the product is ready for release, it is not released. While Pat's team doesn't get everything it requests, it is evaluating test tools and has approval to hire three more people to add to the test team. That's when Joe's day suddenly improves. Better go update that résumé!

In this scenario, Joe and Pat have similar responsibilities and face similar challenges. The main difference that causes Pat to be more effective with a healthier job outlook is that her management understands testing. Pat's management sees the need to support the testing effort not only with funding, but also with the attitude that testing is important and that the product doesn't ship until it is right.

Pat's organization has a different management culture that believes in quality and then acts on those beliefs. This culture looks ahead to projects five and ten years from now. Pat's management knows its customers won't stand for shoddy software and has decided to distinguish its products with outstanding quality.

This management culture also places a high value on people. Instead of dividing the company into competing groups, people are organized into teams that are interdependent on each other for success.

IMPACT ON TESTING

In more than seventy-five percent of the organizations we have surveyed, there is no manager of testing activities. There is no person who is responsible for making sure people have the right tools and processes for testing—or that testing is performed at all! Without a manager or leader of testing, people gravitate toward whatever level of testing seems appropriate for the project at hand. When the deadline arrives, testing is considered complete. Then, when problems occur in production, senior management looks for someone to blame.

An Unsupportive View of Test Management

Just think what would happen to other areas of the organization if such were the case. There would be no manager of software development, no manager of personnel, no manager of sales—in short, nothing would get done. Testing is at an ad hoc level in most organizations because there simply is not the awareness and initiative to make testing an effective process. What happens when management doesn't support testing? Following are some of the repercussions.

- **Testing is seen as a luxury.**

  Testing is quality control for software. Yes, it's true there are deadlines to meet and commitments to keep, but until that magic silver bullet is found, testing is the way software defects are found before the customer finds them. To some software development organizations, it's not a problem if the customers find defects. To those with high-risk applications, like aviation and blood banking, software defects are a major concern. Testing should be considered part of the software development or maintenance process, just as quality control is an integral part of any manufacturing process. Companies that build quality products perform quality control—it's part of the process every step of the way, not a luxury.

- **Testing is viewed as something that can be squeezed in at the last minute.**

  When management schedules testing for the end of a project, it is positioning the project for the worst kind of failure. Major defects found at the end of a project are difficult to isolate and costly to fix, and last-minute repairs can have a ripple effect on other system areas. In addition, the political ramifications of resolving late project defects can be major. For example, a company might not be too pleased that the only solution to poor system performance is to buy another million dollars' worth of hardware.

- **Testing is seen as something that can find all of the defects.**

This attitude is evident when management blames the testers for a defect not found during testing. Paradoxically, management feels that testing is superfluous, yet it depends on it to find all of the defects.

The truth is that there are an astronomical number of possible test cases for most software. For all of the test cases you design, someone else can usually find one more that you did not consider. There are techniques such as early technical inspections that greatly help improve your defect removal percentages, but there is still the chance that defects are lurking in very complex parts of the software. For an interesting discussion of this troubling fact, refer to the *Scientific American* article, "The Risks of Software," cited in the Related Reading section.

- **Testing is perceived as intimidating.**

Another part of the testing challenge is that testing is often seen as an intimidating area. People do not feel comfortable with what they do not understand. This especially holds true for management. When managers take a hands-off approach to testing, they need to be educated in the issues and challenges of testing. The comment most often heard from management is, "Why didn't you test for that?"

Management needs to understand that effective testing is a matter of following basic principles and that support is needed for tools, processes, and people. Without management leading the way, the testing effort will be limited in effectiveness.

- **Human effort is expected to compensate for the lack of test tools.**

Management needs to understand that testing is a precise activity that is often repeated due to changes in the software. Accurate test repeatability can only be accomplished by using automated test tools. When management opts not to acquire tools and instead expects people to perform the same kinds of tests manually, it is trading financial capital for an inefficient use of people's time. In many cases, other teams will get tools, but not the testers.

There are cases when there is no good tool solution. Sometimes, the technical environment or other factors may preclude the use of commercially available test tools. In this case, the only other options are to build your own tools or continue to test manually.

- **The deadline is the main criteria for knowing when testing is complete.**

For many organizations, the deadline is a main factor for considering testing complete. One reason for this is that management sees more importance in delivering something on time than the quality of what is delivered. However, as someone said, "Junk delivered on time is still junk."

Another reason for deadline-driven testing is that testing is unplanned. This is the musical chairs approach—when the music stops, you scramble to find a seat and wait to see who (or "what," in this case) gets left out. People perform whatever testing they can in the allotted time and whatever doesn't get tested is left for the customer to find. A variation on this approach is when testing is planned, but the project schedule does not accommodate the time needed for testing. Making the choice between meeting the deadline and delivering quality software is a major test of management's commitment to quality.

A Strategic View of Test Management

We've looked at the impact of a lack of management support. Now let's take a look at the support framework that is needed to manage testing. You need to be concerned with three areas:

- **Manage toward results.**

  In the context of testing, there should be defined testing criteria that should be met before a product is released to customers. Examples of these criteria would include software requirements that function correctly, software/system performance at specified levels, user acceptance scenarios that function correctly, and so forth.

- **Manage by process.**

  Processes must be in place to establish consistency. Without processes in place, one group of people will be testing one way and another group may be testing in a totally different manner. The result is unpredictable results and varying completion times for testing. Without defined and repeatable processes, testing is a new world every day!

- **Manage with facts.**

  Facts are the measurements obtained during testing that indicate whether the specified goals are being achieved. Examples of facts would be the number of defects found, the defect rate, the number of test cases executed, and so on.

  Facts are obtained from dashboards, much like you use your car's dashboard to tell you how fast you are traveling and how far you have traveled. There are two kinds of dashboards for testing: the strategic dashboard and the tactical dashboard. The strategic dashboard helps you to manage toward results and the tactical dashboard helps you manage by process.

In Figure 6.1, these management components are shown to work together to achieve two purposes: to meet the customers' expectations and the organization's visions and goals.

By examining Figure 6.1, you can see that managing quality activities, such as testing, requires a lot more than just telling someone to go do something. Management must understand this framework to make quality happen.

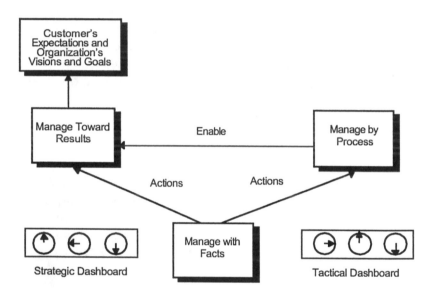

Figure 6.1: The Strategic View of Quality Management—What to Do (© Quality Assurance Institute; reprinted by permission).

SOLUTIONS TO THE CHALLENGE

So far, we have discussed *them*—management—quite a bit. Now, let's look at some practical things you can do to affect change in your organization and to raise management awareness of testing.

First, let's explore the idea that you can mature the testing process only to the extent that senior management matures. To further understand this concept, consider the levels of maturity as portrayed in the Software Engineering Institute's (SEI) Capability Maturity Model^SM (CMM). Although not everyone buys into the CMM, it is still a good framework to understand the phases an organization must go through to excel at software development.

The Quality Assurance Institute has extended the concept to include other areas of the organization that must go through levels of maturity, such as people, management, technology, deliverable, quality assurance, and quality control (see Figure 6.2).

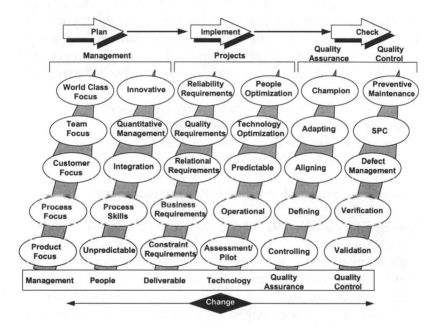

Figure 6.2: Maturing the Six Individual Process Categories
(© Quality Assurance Institute; reprinted by permission).

It is beyond the scope of this chapter and this book to go into detail about all six process tracks shown in Figure 6.2. However, it is important to observe what happens on the management track. The difference between levels 1 and 2, the bottom two levels, is that management moves from a product focus to a process focus. We could also discuss what happens after that, but since most organizations are still at level 1, we will limit the discussion to the transition from product to process.

If you ask managers what their focus is, they will usually tell you it is process, not product. If you look at what actually happens in day-to-day activities, though, the focus is often on the product. You will hear statements like, "We need to get the product out by next month-end," or "We don't have the budget to buy a test tool." These statements focus on product, not process, attributes.

According to Figure 6.2, if you try to mature the testing process while management is focused on the product, you will be fighting an uphill battle. The way organizational maturity should occur in this model is that the management maturity track should lead the rest of the organization by achieving its levels of maturity first.

Now that we have examined why it is important for management to take the lead in organizational change and maturing processes, let's look at some practical things you can do to help management understand testing.

Identify the Stakeholders at the Management Level

Stakeholders are people who have a vested interest in something. Sometimes, the interest is positive, and the stakeholder anticipates a gain. Other times, the interest is negative, and the stakeholder wants to prevent something from happening because he or she predicts a loss. These expectations of gain or loss often relate to a manager's area of control, or turf, as it is sometimes called.

Stakeholders will make or break progress. You must know the management landscape to understand who the stakeholders are. Once you understand who the positive stakeholders are, you can identify one or more champions to help raise testing awareness to their peers in management. It is a good idea to find a champion at a high level in the organization, since that is where major decisions are made. Likewise, once you identify the negative stakeholders, you can shape persuasive messages to address their concerns.

Raise Awareness of the Testing Function

The awareness-raising efforts concern educating people, including management, in the importance of testing and how it can benefit them. Many myths are commonly believed about testing and it will take someone to convey the facts. These common myths of testing include ideas like, "We don't have time to test, so just let the users test the new version," or "The best test is a random test."

Awareness is increased by gradual means. The little things can go a long way in raising awareness. A key is to avoid so much repetition in the message that it becomes ignored. Another key concept is to make the message positive so that you are not seen as a constant complainer.

Some ways to help raise awareness include keeping your positive stakeholders abreast of new developments in testing by passing magazine or newsletter articles, conducting learn-at-lunch sessions for all people in the organization, and tactfully using the teachable moment of software failure to show what could have been done to prevent the defect from occurring in production. Some people have found that external consultants are sometimes needed to be brutally honest with senior management and make the message that no one else dares to say.

Network with Other Organizations to Learn How They Deal with Management

If you speak with people in other organizations, you will quickly learn that you are not alone when it comes to many of the issues in testing. Look for organizations with a proactive quality culture and find out what they did to make it happen. Unfortunately, these organizations are in the minority, so you might need to look hard to find them.

Establish a Testing Charter to Define the Purpose of Testing in Your Organization

One reason that management doesn't know the exact purpose of testing is that testing has never been officially defined in the organization. A testing charter outlines specifically what testing is expected to accomplish. For example, the testing charter will define whether the purpose of testing is to find defects or to prove correctness. The testing charter should also indicate who performs testing and how the results of testing are reported.

Define Measurable Testing Objectives

Testing metrics are beyond the scope of this book, but they are essential to your success. You will need a way to measure your success and that measurement should make sense. These measurements are represented by the dashboard in Figure 6.1 (see page 82). Without a way to measure progress, you will never know how well you are doing and neither will management. The tricky thing about measurement is finding the right thing to measure. You have probably heard the adage, "You get what you measure." For example, if the number of defects found is the measure of testing success, then the more defects we find, the better we look. The problem is that all of those defects are expensive to fix. We can look good according to the measure, even while our performance is dysfunctional.

Dedicate a Manager of Testing Who Understands the Issues and Challenges

There are two parts to this suggestion. First, as discussed earlier, make testing a managed activity. Second, the manager should understand testing. The test manager should be trained in testing techniques and should stay current in the field. This understanding is essential for testing to become an effective process in an organization.

Table 6.1 shows essential testing support tasks by levels of management. If you are having trouble because testing is ineffective in your organization, benchmark your level of management support against Table 6.1 and you will find the gaps. These gaps will show you where to focus your awareness-raising efforts.

Table 6.1.
Levels of Testing Responsibility.

Responsibility \ Management Level	Senior Management	Middle Management	Project/Team Leaders
Understand the importance of testing in terms of business risk	X	X	X
Understand the importance of mature processes	X	X	X
Promote testing efforts visibly	X	X	X
Make critical decisions of time and budget vs. quality	X	X	
Define a vision for what testing should accomplish		X	X
Lead in acquiring testing tools, training, and services		X	X
Lead in developing testing processes		X	X
Lead in controlling testing processes		X	X
Lead in performing testing processes			X
Lead in the measurement of testing results			X
Lead in the continuous improvement of testing processes			X

Make Testing a Process

When testing is a process, people know what to test, when to test, who should test, and what the success criteria are. A testing process can be managed, measured, and repeated. The alternative to having a testing process is inconsistent, random, and unpredictable testing that results in low levels of software quality and high levels of rework.

Is process definition easy? By no means! Many organizations have found it a very difficult task, requiring the dedication and support of the entire organization.

Is process definition beneficial? Absolutely! The key to having a beneficial process is to define a process that is effective. Of course, it is possible to have a process that delivers results that miss quality success criteria. The challenge is to develop testing processes that are appropriate for the people in your organization.

SOLUTION IMPEDIMENTS

What if management is satisfied with the status quo, since we've done well in the past with ad hoc testing?

As in other areas of life, people are not motivated to change the status quo unless there is great pain or great benefit. There are some things to realize about this situation:

- Ad hoc testing is risky, so make management aware of the risks to the business and to the customer.
- Ad hoc testing is costly, although the perception is just the opposite. The defects that are found in production cost about one hundred times more than those found early in the project.
- Testing is quality control. Is your management willing to trust the quality of the products and services delivered to random methods?

Ultimately, the degree of testing is determined by management, since it sets the schedule and makes the budget. If management is satisfied with random and haphazard testing, it is basically blessing a risky quality control method. The corporate landscape is riddled with the remains of those who made the same erroneous blessing.

What if we can't find a champion for testing?

Keep making your message and hope that a spark ignites a flame. Everyone reaches realization in stages, although sometimes it seems as if it is an overnight event. Overnight conversions often result from many repetitions of a message.

How do I find other organizations with which to network and benchmark?

In most major metropolitan areas across the United States, there are local organizations dedicated to exchanging information about software quality. A list of some of those organizations appears in the Resources section of this book. Some local quality assurance groups also have Web pages.

You can also attend testing and software quality conferences. These conferences address important testing and software quality topics and are a good way to meet people who share many of your concerns.

GUIDELINES FOR SUCCESS

- **Be patient. Raising management awareness of testing can take a long time.**

The exception is when a crisis situation, such as a major software or system failure, causes management to scramble to improve quality by way of testing. Many times, the crisis motivation is short-lived and interest will fade away until the next crisis.

- **Quality is ultimately management's responsibility.**

  Dr. Deming said it best: "Quality is everybody's business, but it's management's responsibility."

- **Focus your message to management on cost and time.**

  The key motivators for management are saving money and delivering software faster.

- **Meeting the schedule is not the only measure of success.**

  "The bitterness of poor quality remains long after the sweetness of meeting the schedule has been forgotten."
  —Motto of the Quality Assurance Institute

- **Measure and publicize your efforts.**

  Successful testing organizations know how many defects they found last week, last month, and last year. These organizations make sure their management is aware of the money saved by finding these defects.

- **Marketing is part of your job. Learn how to market well.**

  "If you just communicate, you can get by. But if you skillfully communicate, you can work miracles."
  —Jim Rohn

PLAN OF ACTION

Although each organization is different in terms of culture and management structure, the following basic steps can be applied and/or adapted to increase the level of management understanding and awareness of testing in your organization.

1. Develop a testing charter. First, *you* must understand what the purpose of testing in your organization is.

2. Identify the stakeholders. At this point, also identify the people who will help champion this effort.

3. Identify your target market. Much of your effort will be in marketing and in selling management on what testing really is and the value of testing. Just as in marketing any product or service, you must focus on the benefits to your customer. One approach is to target the high percentage of undecided or unaware people. Avoid spending much time on strong opponents or supporters.

4. Define your strategy and objectives. This sets the direction of your efforts, now that you know the players and the message you want to make.

5. Assess your current condition. This can be done in a self-assessment, such as the one in Chapter 2, or in consultation with an outside person who has testing expertise. This assessment will be the baseline against which your progress will be measured.

6. Start making the message. Awareness raising can assume many forms, such as newsletters, learn-at-lunch sessions, and distribution of magazine articles.

7. Keep making the message. Awareness raising never ends. In fact, if you stop making the message, the overall level of awareness will probably revert back to its original level.

CHAPTER SEVEN

CHALLENGE #6: COMMUNICATING WITH CUSTOMERS—AND USERS

OVERVIEW

"Why doesn't this %$@# system work?" is an often-heard phrase, right along with, "Please be patient with us. We just installed a new computer system." Does this make sense? Isn't the purpose of all this technology to make work easier, not harder? Not if you talk to the typical information system end-user.

The system users will tell you what it's like in the trenches when a system misses the mark. You will hear stories about piles of paperwork because the system is too slow to process the normal daily work load. You will hear about processes that used to be efficient before the new system was installed.

Why does this happen? One major reason is that the customer and users of the system are not known, understood, or involved in the system development or purchase process. In this chapter, we explore the impact of this lack of involvement and how to increase customer and user involvement in the delivery of information systems.

STATE OF THE PRACTICE

The project is in the prototyping stage and already behind schedule. What was supposed to be finished two months ago is still going through cycles of change. Sue, the project manager, complains that "the users keep changing their minds." The end-users complain that the developers "just don't get it." And so, on it goes, with the prototyping process continuing without a final agreement on what the software should do.

Contributing to the problem is the fact that even the end-users can't seem to agree on what the system should do. Some of the users in one region of the country want one set of features, while other users feel *their* desired features are more important. In this case, the customer, who is the director of sales, hasn't even spoken to the development manager since the first day of the project.

Many of the users are skeptical about the new project because they are very comfortable with the old system and do not understand why it is being replaced. The system users are very busy with running a business and feel they do not have the time to contribute to the new system effort.

The testers on the project are concerned because they know the system should undergo a period of user acceptance testing, but they don't know whose criteria will form the basis of that testing. If the users can't reach consensus on the prototype, how in the world will they ever agree on acceptance criteria or be motivated to conduct an acceptance test for a system they do not really want?

In this case study, there are several key factors that are placing the project at risk:

- The prototyping process is not controlled.
- There is a breakdown of communication.
- The business users are not sold on the idea of having a new system.
- The users do not want to be involved in the system development and testing process.

IMPACT ON TESTING

When the customer is not clearly identified and involved in testing, the final product is at great risk of missing the business or operational need completely. Identifying the customer is essential long before testing. How can the right system be built if the developers aren't talking to the right people?

That's the challenge: discerning the customer from the end-user and gaining agreement in spite of any political issues that may arise. A good example of the difference between the customer and the user is evident in a toy store. If you have ever purchased a toy for a child, you may have learned that what you like and what the child likes can be two entirely different things. It is not uncommon for a child to spend more time playing with the toy's packaging than with the toy itself.

Please don't misinterpret this example as portraying system users as children—that's not the point. The point is that the people sponsoring the project (the customers) and the people benefiting from the system (the end-users) each have their own sets of success and failure criteria.

Customers and end-users can be either internal or external to your organization, depending on whether your company deploys systems in-house or develops software for the commercial market. Internal customers and end-users have a different set of concerns from external customers and end-users. Internal customers and users are concerned about the success of the project and how it affects the success of the organization and their role in the organization. They are naturally concerned with the quality of the project because it can directly affect their work life. Also, internal customers and users usually have a history and a foreseeable future in a relationship with the developers of the system.

External customers and users can be swayed by competition and market forces. Many software companies know the levels of quality their customers will accept. If the level of quality drops, or if a competitor's product has a lower price or more features, external customers may switch to the competitor. Internal customers and users do not have this luxury, in most cases.

When the real customer or user is not identified on a project,

- the project can fail
- the system may be unusable
- the system development costs can soar out of control
- the software company can lose competitive advantage or market share
- the system may be more of a hindrance than a help to the organization

There is a second, very important issue of end-user involvement in testing: It varies greatly from organization to organization. Some organizations view user acceptance testing as just a ritual that must be performed—without the users knowing enough about the system to really test it—so the users give the system a cursory look and bless it.

Other organizations view user acceptance testing as the only form of testing performed on a project. In this case, the testing is rigorous and the users take on more than their share of the testing responsibility.

At both extremes just discussed, the end-user testers are not used effectively. When the system users are not involved at an optimal level in testing,

- the system may work according to written requirements, but not in the real world
- parts of the system may be tested complete, but the system as a whole might not work correctly
- users may lack confidence in using the system
- users may not use the system correctly

There are two major issues concerning the customer/end-user role in testing. First, has the customer been defined and is the user community in agreement with the project's goals and objectives? Second, do the customers and end-users understand and accept their role in system development (or system purchase) and testing?

SOLUTIONS TO THE CHALLENGE

First, let's examine the customers' and end-users' role in system development or purchase and in testing. Table 7.1 shows the roles for each group.

Table 7.1.
Customer and End-User Project Roles.

Group	Roles
Customers	• Project sponsors • Understand end-user needs and issues • Provide high-level requirements to software developers/vendors • Alpha/beta testing
End-Users	• Eventual users of the system • Understand business/operation needs of the system • Provide detailed requirements to software developers/vendors • Design and conduct user acceptance testing • Alpha/beta testing

Table 7.2, The Testing Roles of Customers and End-Users During a Project, shows the roles of the customers and end-users as they relate to the testing activities on a project. It is obvious from Table 7.2 that the customers' and end-users' role in testing is not limited to the end of the process, but rather should extend throughout the system development process. If the context of your projects is primarily system maintenance, the same basic project tasks should be performed, but on a smaller scale. If you are responsible for testing purchased software, your customers and end-users should be heavily

The Testing Roles of Customers and End-Users During a Project.

Project Phase / Test Activity	Project Initiation	Requirements Definition	Prototyping	System Design	System Construction	Functional Testing
Test Planning						Acceptance test cases, Defining acceptance test criteria
Test Execution	Feasibility reviews, Cost/benefit analysis	Requirements review	Prototype review	Design review		Acceptance testing
Test Evaluation	Evaluate if the system solution will meet business or operational needs.	Evaluate review results to determine accuracy of requirements—i.e., has the right system been specified?	Evaluate the correctness of the prototype to meet business or operational needs.	Evaluate the system design for support of requirements. At a general level of detail, does the design appear to support the original user requirements?	Evaluate the system deliverables in stages to determine if the right system is being built.	Evaluate the acceptance testing results to determine if acceptance criteria has been met—i.e., was the right system delivered?
Test Reporting	Produce feasibility analysis report.	Produce requirements review report.	Produce prototyping status report(s).	Produce design review report.	Produce system construction status report(s).	Produce acceptance testing status report(s) and final acceptance testing report.

involved in the specification of system requirements and product evaluations. When purchased systems are customized or have a high risk, a rigorous acceptance test should be performed.

The solutions to identifying the customer and the user and meeting their needs depend on three basic concepts: teamwork, communication, and continuous involvement. When one of these three elements is lacking, the customer and end-user will not be effectively involved in ensuring that the system delivered is the right system.

Teamwork

In some organizational cultures, there is distrust between the system developers and the customer. In fact, in some organizations, the end-users do not trust the system developer or the sponsoring customers. To establish a teamwork attitude, people must trust each other. This is tough when there is a history of violated trust. Once trust is broken, it is hard to restore.

Perhaps an agreement between the customer and the system development group was broken some time ago. The developers are subsequently reluctant to believe what the customer tells them. Alternatively, the customer or sponsor misrepresents or fails to represent the needs of the end-users. When this happens, the end-users feel betrayed and frustrated because they must live with a system that does not meet their needs. An often-heard comment from end-users is, "I just wish we had the old system back."

The underlying solution to all of this is deceptively simple, so here it is in several interpretations: be consistent; be honest; be direct; be congruent;[1] be trustworthy. Without trust, you don't have a team—you have a group.

Communication

Let's imagine that you want to build the house of your dreams. You've worked and saved for years, and now you finally have

---

[1] For a discussion of congruence, see Gerald M. Weinberg, *Quality Software Management, Vol. 3: Congruent Action* (New York: Dorset House Publishing, 1994).

the funds to build your castle. You contact the architect and tell him you want a house. Then you go away. Six months later you close on the deal, move in, and live happily ever after, right? Not on your life!

You can see from this example the impossibility of only being involved at the beginning and the end of a project. In the case of the house, there are many decisions to be made along the way and you, the customer, need to know exactly what is going on, how much the house will cost, and when the builder expects to finish. Every step involves necessary communication.

Why is it that in system projects customers are content to stay out of the communication loop until the end? One reason is that the customer and the end-users do not know precisely what they want any more than a prospective homeowner can tell the architect every detail of his dream house. However, with skilled guidance, the customer can become involved by discussing what is feasible and realistic.

Another reason the customer may avoid communication is that the system developers speak their own language. All the customer is concerned with is "Will it work for the business?" Never mind about the DLLs, the servers, and the other technical jargon.

There seems to be a built-in communication gap between technical people and business people. It's tough for technical people who deal in minute details all day to summarize the big picture, just as it's hard for big-picture people to think in terms of minute details. People who can fluently switch from the big picture to the technical detail are the exception, but are desperately needed to keep the communication open on a project.

Communication problems with customers and end-users are so complex—especially during testing—that solutions are sometimes hard to find. Keeping that fact in mind, try the following basic and practical approaches that have worked for other people.

- **Keep talking, even if it means disagreeing.**

  About the worst thing that can happen on a project is when the eventual users of the system and the sponsors of the system are in the dark as to what is going on with building the system. Constant communication is what keeps surprises at a minimum.

  A common tendency is to avoid communication when people disagree. Although disagreements are sometimes difficult to work through, they should not cut off communication.

- **Don't confuse meetings, memos, and e-mail with effective communication.**

  Meetings, memos, and e-mail are vehicles of communication, but they are not the message. You can write twenty e-mail messages to the same person in one day and perhaps convey the wrong message completely. In addition, communication is not only *what* you say, but *how* you say it. Some organizations actually encourage their employees to take frequent breaks together because it facilitates informal communication, which is vital to a project.

- **If there is a communication barrier, seek help from the services of a facilitator.**

  Sometimes, the communication levels in an organization have deteriorated to the extent that outside help is needed to bridge the gap between users, customers, and developers. Like a marriage counselor, a facilitator can help identify key issues and keep communication alive if the parties are willing to communicate on at least a basic level.

Continuous Involvement

There are two sides to the issue of continuous customer and end-user involvement on a project:

1. The customer and the end-users want to be involved, but project management prefers otherwise.
2. Project management wants the customer and the end-users to be involved throughout the project, but they prefer otherwise.

Both scenarios place the project at a disadvantage, and there are no easy answers to motivate people toward shared involvement. For continuous customer and end-user involvement to become a reality, the following attitudes must prevail:

- Information Systems management or project management must provide a structure (preferably a process) for continuous involvement.
- Information Systems management or project management must issue an invitation for customers and users to become involved in the project. Gate crashing just isn't effective.
- Senior management must support and perhaps even dictate that the customer and end-user be involved in the project. After all, it might only be the business at stake.
- End-users and the customer must understand the benefits of the project and why their involvement is crucial to the success of the project. The end-users also need to understand that the project may be critical to the success of the business.

Without continuous customer and end-user involvement on the project, major objectives can be missed, which leads to disappointment and customer dissatisfaction. This occurrence is called "the expectation gap" (Figure 7.1).

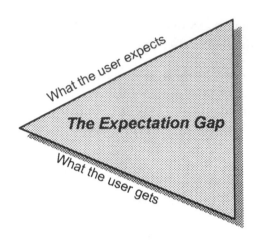

Figure 7.1: The Expectation Gap.

One of the problems with user acceptance testing is that it often occurs at the very end of the system delivery process. The end of the project is the worst time to find out that the system will not meet the business or operational needs of the end-users. The solution is continuous involvement in the project to mini-mize the expectation gap.

User Acceptance Testing

As mentioned earlier, there are many differing views of user acceptance testing. In recent years, the popularity of user acceptance testing has increased as end-users have become more involved in the software and system development arena. A problem is that not only is the purpose of user acceptance testing misunderstood, but the techniques are not widely taught, either.

In the case of external customers and users, beta testing is a popular way to test when customer and user involvement is not feasible or practical. Like many forms of testing, beta test-ing has its pros and cons. On the plus side, beta testing can give insight into how the software will work in real-life situations, and you don't have to pay the testers. In some cases, they even pay you!

The drawbacks to beta testing are that it is risky to the customer and users; there is no control over the testing; the information from beta testing may be unreliable; early defects can result in negative publicity; and fixing defects identified during beta testing can be very expensive. If there is one thing that research of software defects over the past twenty-five to thirty years has discovered, it's that a defect can cost ten to one hundred times more to fix in production than in the early phases of system development. Another problem with beta testing arises when it is relied upon for most of the testing effort. Releasing software for beta testing before your own testing (alpha testing) has been completed is risky for both the software developer and the customer, and this should be avoided. As we have emphasized throughout this book, you should not depend on someone else to do all of the testing for you.

If you refer back to the "V" diagram in Figure 3.1 (see page 35), you will notice that system testing validates requirements. The question to be answered by system testing is, "Was the system built according to requirements?" That's all well and good, but what if the requirements were misinterpreted by the developers? In that case, you might have a system that works on paper but not in the business or operational environment.

The impetus for a system project or purchase is the identification of a need for the system. The system is envisioned to meet a business or operational need. Figure 3.1 shows that the business need is validated by acceptance testing. The question to be answered by user acceptance testing is, "Will the system meet the business or operational needs in the real world?"

A basic mistake made by many people is to base acceptance testing on system requirements. This is, in effect, performing a second independent system test. An acceptance test should be based on business processes or other real-world scenarios. By the time the system is ready for acceptance testing, functional testing based on requirements and specifications should have already been performed by developers and/or independent testers. This should free the end-user to focus on testing the big picture of how the system will perform to meet the originally envisioned need.

The nuts and bolts of user acceptance testing is beyond the scope of this book. However, the basic process should consist of identifying all the business processes to be tested, decomposing those processes to the lowest level of complexity, and testing real-life test cases (people or things) through those processes. This process is like a water pipe. The process is the pipe, which might take many bends and split off in different directions. The test cases, supported by test data, are the water that flows through the pipe. The idea is to design an acceptance test that validates how various test cases will be handled as they pass through many different parts of the system, and even on to other systems.

SOLUTION IMPEDIMENTS

What if the end-users just don't want to be involved in building or testing the system?

When users do not want to be involved with the system, stress the fact that one day it will be a big part of their work lives. They can have a say in the decisions early in the project, or they can lose their right to complain—forever. The choice is theirs.

You can also recruit people who are interested and want to enhance their value to the company. One of the best ways to learn the entire system before anyone else is to be involved in the development and testing of it. End-users are often promoted rapidly from the ranks simply because they are among the few who understand how to use the new system.

What if the end-users have an adversarial attitude toward the developers?

This situation usually requires an independent facilitator to get the two sides together. An adversarial attitude is usually ingrained in the culture of an organization and is not quickly or easily changed. Other skills, such as team building, might need to be learned before the two groups are ready to work together on the project.

What if the project management rejects the idea of customer and end-user involvement?

In this case, the project management is on a very slippery slope. The tacit directive is, "You will take what we give you and you'll either like it or learn to live with it." The focus is not on the customer; it's on the product. If the product proves unable to function in the business, the closed-door attitude toward development can come back to haunt the project management. The revised theme might be, "Good-bye Information Systems, hello outsourcing."

Project management, under the direction of a steering committee or similar body, needs to ensure that key people have a voice in the project.

What if the end-users do not understand technical issues or know how to perform acceptance testing?

If the people are willing to learn, they can be trained. Don't be too eager to discount the users for lack of technical knowledge. The value they bring to the project is a vast knowledge of the business. Don't try to make the end-users techies, just show them how to use and test the system.

GUIDELINES FOR SUCCESS

• **Communicate tactfully.**

> *"Tact is the knack of making a point without making an enemy."*
> —Howard W. Newton

- Lighten up a little. Life will still go on after the project is over.

   "A merry heart doeth good like a medicine."
   —Proverbs 17:22

- You can't please everyone.

   "I don't know the key to success, but the key to failure is to try to please everyone."
   —Bill Cosby

PLAN OF ACTION

1. Start educating the development management and end-user management on the importance of identifying the customer and the end-users.

2. Include customer and end-user tasks in your system development and testing methodologies.

3. Pilot the process. If possible, select a small, lower-risk project to try out user involvement.

4. Train the users in performing their tasks. The training should include how to work with developers to convey requirements, how to evaluate a prototype, and how to design and conduct an effective user acceptance test.

5. Measure the results. Focus on measures of end-user involvement, acceptance criteria test coverage, acceptance testing costs, and defects found during acceptance testing and production.

CHAPTER EIGHT

CHALLENGE #5:
MAKING TIME FOR TESTING

OVERVIEW

Testing is a paradox. If we could just test the parts of the system that we suspect of having defects, we could drastically reduce the amount of time spent on testing; but defects are usually found in the places we least suspect—so we dare not assume that any area of the system is defect-free. As they say, a good tester always looks both ways before crossing a one-way street.

If all areas of the system are suspect for defects, it follows that all areas of the system should be tested. But, to what *extent* should the system be tested? When you consider all of the possible input combinations, there is an astronomical number of test cases required. This leads us to a basic realization about testing: When brute force is used, there is always more work than we could ever possibly complete. No matter how many tests you design and perform, there always seems to be one more. The exception is software that is very small in scope and complexity, which is a rarity in the real world.

Many times, the testing schedule is a "best guess" added to the end of a project to meet an arbitrary deadline. Instead of estimating the testing schedule based on the number of test cases to be performed, the size of the system, or the number of requirements to be tested, the estimate is based on some fuzzy idea of what seems reasonable. Testers are then put under pressure to meet a testing schedule that is severely underestimated.

There are also variations on this theme, such as the situation when there is no major project, only continuous maintenance, as in legacy systems. In that case, independent testers are expected to keep up with the work of developers. Many times, this work load can be overwhelming and the pressure to complete the test can be relentless.

An interesting question is, "What would happen if management gave testers all the time they needed for testing?" Probably, there would still not be enough time for what many people consider complete testing. Somewhere between the agony of rushed deadlines and the luxury of all the time in the world has got to be a reasonable approach to testing. That's what the rest of this chapter is all about—making the most of the time you have available.

STATE OF THE PRACTICE

Joe and Mary are members of the testing organization at Fantastic Foods, a large corporation managing hundreds of grocery stores. Joe is on a major project to develop a new data warehousing system, and Mary is working on an independent test team to test changes made to the company's twenty-year-old inventory system.

One day at lunch, Joe and Mary discover that although they are working on two totally separate and unrelated projects, they share a common problem: too many things to test and not enough time to test them. "It just seems like the project schedule was based on the deadline—as if we could fit in all the work," observed Joe. "This project is so large and complex, I don't know how we'll ever get any level of confidence that the system really works. My management just says to test everything we have time to test, but at the same time, they say that the department's reputation rests on this project. It's like we're in an impossible situation, yet nobody wants to admit it," Joe said.

Mary agreed, "Yeah, I don't know how much longer I can stand getting the same programs to test over and over. What's worse is that the defects seem to be getting worse instead of better. I got one program yesterday at ten A.M. that had to be tested by three P.M. The regular test takes over twelve hours to run! Tell me, how do I keep doing this without sacrificing the quality of the test?"

The problems that Joe and Mary face in this scenario are

- **They expect themselves to test everything.**

  Although everyone at Fantastic Foods understands that the systems under test are complex, no one seems to transfer this understanding to testing. This inconsistent expectation is even held by the testers. Because everything is fair game for testing, there is no effort to define or control the scope of testing.

- **Their management expects them to test everything.**

  To their credit, the managers understand the need for quality control (testing) on the system projects at Fantastic Foods. However, increased awareness of the dynamics of testing large and complex systems is needed. In this case, management should be leading the effort in defining a risk-based process for specifying and controlling the scope of testing. Until management understands that it is impossible to test everything, there will likely be a false assertion of blame on the testers if a defect is found by a customer or user, usually in the form of "I thought you guys were supposed to be testing this system. How did you miss this problem?"

- **There is not enough time to test everything.**

  If you examine the project schedule and the delivery process for changes to the legacy system, you will see that a set amount of time is defined for testing. We call this allotted time "the box." The challenge that testers have is to fit their testing into the box, and sometimes the box gets smaller if other parts of the project fall behind schedule. Realizing what is really going on in terms of time helps people to set more realistic expectations of what can be accomplished.

  Let's be more specific as to what is or is not reasonable in terms of test objectives. What is not reasonable is to expect to test every random combination of events or paths in an average software module. Even if you could completely test all combinations in one module, the complexity explodes when a second or third module is introduced. What is reasonable is to use an approach like requirements-based testing to pinpoint the test cases you need to perform. This approach can reduce the number of test cases in some instances from hundreds of thousands to less than one hundred.

- **The testing estimates are not based on any kind of measurable criteria.**

  Not only do the estimates fail to define or to control the scope of testing, the estimates for testing are not based on anything measurable. This reinforces the ineffective technique of fitting testing into the allotted time—regardless of whether or not the testing is effective. The reason that estimates are only best guesses stems from the fact that the measurable criteria are not available until later in the project. The good news is that there are ways to get measurable criteria early in the project.

IMPACT ON TESTING

The quality of testing is not so much determined by how much testing is performed or how fast testing is performed, but rather by *what* is tested. When there is a rush to get the product to the customer, the temptation (and often the practice) is to shortcut testing. When testing is rushed or arbitrarily reduced in scope, defects are missed by the testers but easily found by the customers and users of the software.

The key to reducing this negative impact is to design tests based on risk, without the intention of validating every possible combination of inputs and actions. In other words, pick your test cases carefully and design a test that is achievable. If we understand the complexity of systems, it is easy to see that there must be a better way to test software than the brute force method of trying all of the combinations. In Figure 8.1, you can see how the complexity of the test increases as the phases of testing become more encompassing. At the unit testing level, it is not impossible to completely test a single unit, but when you combine units and consider all of the possible interactions between them, the complexity starts to expand. At the system test level, the complexity is too large to test completely.

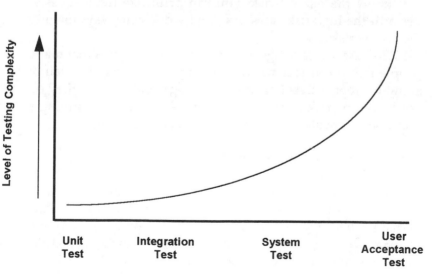

Figure 8.1: Complexity Increases as Testing Progresses.

111

Don't be discouraged: The point is that to have enough time to perform an effective test, you must design a test based on an independent set of criteria, as opposed to a test of every possible combination of input. Possible criteria can include requirements, business processes, and business cases or scenarios.

When too much testing is attempted within the allotted time, testing exhibits the following characteristics:

- reduced test coverage
- increased risk of regression defects
- fatigue, burnout, and low morale

Let's examine the nature of each of these impacts on testing.

Reduced Test Coverage

Test coverage gets reduced when test cases are skipped for the sake of time. One could make a convincing argument that since you can't test everything anyway, why not toss out a few test cases? The key is in knowing the relative risk of the functions or attributes that the test cases are to test. The risk of the software functions is determined in a risk assessment. When you know the relative risk, you can prioritize the test cases, perform the high risk cases first, and work your way down to the lowest risk cases.

Reduced test coverage brings to light two factors that many people fail to consider when planning tests. First, they fail to allow for repeat tests (regression testing), and second, they do not know the risk of the functions to be tested. Performing a risk assessment should be a part of every testing process.

Increased Risk of Regression Defects

We have already discussed that you can only reasonably test a subset of all possible test cases, so what does this mean? Perhaps a better way to visualize this concept is with a graph of what typically happens during a rushed testing schedule. The diagram of manual testing in Chapter 5 (see Figure 5.1 on page 61) shows that testing takes place at the very end of the project. This "big bang" approach to testing can be relieved a great deal by continuous verification and validation throughout a project.

In Figure 5.1, a noble effort is made to completely test all cases each time a new release of the software is received from the developers. All goes well until the testers burn out by testing the software manually. As the deadline approaches (and passes), the work keeps coming, and the degree of testing is gradually compromised until only the changes are tested. This exposes the project to those nasty defects that get introduced as the result of fixing another defect: regression defects. In effect, the quality and the degree of testing are sacrificed to meet the deadline.

One way to deal with the scenario shown in Figure 5.1 is to automate testing. This solution is not a silver bullet, however. Groundwork must be laid in terms of process and people before the tool will be effective, as discussed in Chapter 5. Figure 5.2 (see page 61) shows that automated testing, like manual testing, requires a significant investment at the beginning to create test scripts and test cases, but the payback comes as those tests are repeated and verified by the automated test tool. Because the time required to repeat an automated test is much shorter than that for the original manual test, regression testing can be performed more times.

If you are currently using automated test tools effectively in your organization, you may be puzzled by our focus on manual testing. We have found that many people are still using manual methods and are struggling to maximize their test time. Automated testing helps you to leverage your time. However, the challenge remains to test the right conditions, as opposed to as many conditions as possible.

Fatigue, Burnout, and Low Morale

One of the most common results of trying to do too much testing in a given time is for people to simply give out or give up. Many of the testers who attend our seminars report that they work in shifts and on weekends just to keep up with the developers. Part of the problem might be management's perception of testing. If the perception is that testing should be quick, easy, and performed by anyone with at least two fingers with which to type, then management will probably not be expecting burnout and low morale. Even if management has the attitude that long hours are part of the territory, the fact remains that tired, burned-out people are not very attentive to finding defects.

SOLUTIONS TO THE CHALLENGE

Control the Scope of Testing

It only makes sense that when it comes to testing, you should not bite off more than you can chew. A good way to define the scope of testing is to relate test objectives to system or project objectives. There should be a one-to-one correspondence between what the system should do or be and what should be tested. It might take many tests to validate a system objective, but all tests should point back to a major test objective.

Control Management Expectations

We need to manage expectations in all project areas, but especially in testing. When pressured into a last-minute "rush job," some testers estimate what percentage of a complete test can be performed and ask management, "Which parts do you want me to test?" This can be a shock to some managers who expect you to work through the night to test that ultra-important last-minute project. However, it does raise awareness that testing is not just a quick, afterthought job.

Base Test Cases on an Independent Set of Criteria

One of the most common complaints from testers under pressure is that there are no defined requirements. The result of having no requirements is that testers (and everyone else, for that matter) are left to their own devices in determining what the system is supposed to do. The chances are slim that everyone's expectations will be the same. You need some kind of evaluation criteria to determine what to test and whether or not the test was successful. If you have no evaluation criteria and no way to measure the results, why bother with testing a specific function? With limited time available, you should focus testing on those functions that can be measured.

Perform Risk Assessments

With only so much time available for testing, you need some way to rank testing activities. Risk is the perfect criteria for prioritizing items to be tested, test cases to be performed, and the like. There are several risk assessments in the public domain that address risk from the project perspective. You can perform risk assessment on an informal basis using likelihood of failure and impact of failure as ranking criteria.

Reuse Your Testware

When time available for test planning and testing is at a premium, you should design test products (such as test plans, test scripts, and test data) that can be used in future tests of the same software, or as templates for future projects. When creating reusable testware, make sure the scripts are modular and that standards exist for the format of test products. Also, take care to keep the test scripts free of detailed test data. The advantage of keeping the test scripts and test data separate is that you have fewer scripts to maintain, plus you can design many different tests simply by combining scripts and data in different ways. In addition, modular test products greatly facilitate the transition to automated testing.

In Figure 8.2, three simple test scripts are combined in different ways. The three scripts are *add* a customer, *change* a customer, and *delete* a customer. These three scripts become the source for several tests. This is a very different approach from writing a single script for testing all three functions.

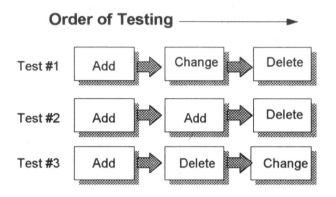

Figure 8.2: Modular Test Script Usage.

Estimate the Testing Effort Based on Measurable Criteria

Instead of using near-random time estimates of the number of weeks required for testing, base your estimates on the number of test cases, system size, testable requirements, and other measurable criteria. Then you will have information on hand to support your estimates. Try tracking test times and using the historical information as a basis for future estimates. Testable requirements are a good basis for early estimates because they don't deal with lines of code, number of modules, and so forth.

Use Automation

This solution appears last in this list to emphasize the point that test automation is important but not the only option in dealing with heavy work loads. The temptation is to bring in a test tool at a crisis moment, but this is seldom effective—in reality, more than a tool solution is usually required. When used as part of an overall testing process, with trained people, automated test tools can be a great help to testers and developers alike. A test that might take days to perform can be performed in minutes with an automated test tool.

SOLUTION IMPEDIMENTS

What if my management refuses to acknowledge the need for better estimates, test tools, or any of the other solutions you suggest?

Remember that "It's their job, their business, and their profits." Many people erroneously think that testing is a technical decision. Only a small part of testing is technical. The larger and more important part is business-oriented. Testing is what controls the quality of the product delivered to your customers and to your end-users. In business, poor quality will lose customers quickly, especially in a competitive marketplace. If your management is willing to take that risk, it's their responsibility, and it's out of your control as a tester. Unfortunately, a decision to release poor-quality software can affect the fortunes of everyone if the company fails.

What if I do not have measurable criteria, such as requirements, to serve as the basis of my tests?

There are a couple of options to try. One is to reverse-engineer the requirements from your working knowledge of the system. Yes, it may seem weird, and at times you will feel like you are violating good practice—like painting a target wherever the arrow hits. This does, however, set a standard that can be estimated and benchmarked against. You might be surprised at how many people will be interested in seeing the reverse-engineered requirements to understand what the system is really supposed to do.

Another technique is to perform an exploratory test applying your sense of how the software should work. In effect, you are using the system as a prospective end-user would. This is difficult because your perception of how the system should work may be totally different from the design; the defects you find might not be defects at all, but you still have to assess them. All in all, this is a weak and unreliable form of testing. But then again, not defining requirements is also a weak and unreliable way to build a system!

How do I control the scope of a test if the scope is constantly changing?

A *scope creep* is a contingency that should be considered in the test plan. You should have plans for at least a ten percent increase in the scope of work. Many times you will not be able to control the amount of software to be tested, but you can control the amount of testing performed on software. One very helpful approach is the "build" technique, in which successive builds of the system are tested. Each version of the software or system has an increased level of functionality over the previous build, much like stair steps (see Figure 8.3).

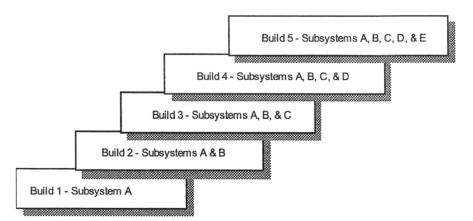

Build 5 - Subsystems A, B, C, D, & E

Build 4 - Subsystems A, B, C, & D

Build 3 - Subsystems A, B, & C

Build 2 - Subsystems A & B

Build 1 - Subsystem A

Figure 8.3: The Build Technique.

What is a common ratio of testers to developers?

There may not be a "common" ratio. In fact, we don't think this is a good way to benchmark your testing effort. First of all, technologies and testing techniques differ from organization to organization. Second, to assume everyone else is testing effectively is a huge leap. Third, suppose the answer you arrive at for your organization is ten times the size of your current testing staff. Could you get the funding to hire that many new people? If so, could you manage them?

A reasonable starting point is to determine how many people you can effectively manage and with whom you can maintain good communication. Then assign duties within that group that align with your testing responsibilities. For example, two people might perform regression testing, one person might perform stress testing, and so forth. Within that framework, develop a set of testing techniques, tools, and standards (in short, a test process) that will streamline the testing effort. Studies have proven that small teams with even a shred of a common process can outperform large teams, simply due to the decreased complexity of communication.

GUIDELINES FOR SUCCESS

- **Remember: Work expands to fill available time.**

  Few tests are completed ahead of schedule, but many projects are extended because of problems found at the end. Considering the effect of secondary testing, such as regression tests, it is possible to see how a two-week test can easily turn into a four- or six-week test.

- **Have a plan—and plan for the unexpected.**

  Count on the possibility that you will need to perform regression testing, or that a new version of the software will be delivered in the middle of the test, and so forth.

> *"He who every morning plans the transaction of the day and follows out the plan carries a thread that will guide him through the labyrinth of the most busy life. . . . But where no plan is laid, where the disposal of time is surrendered merely to the chance of incidents, chaos will soon reign."*
> —Victor Hugo

- **Control your scope.**

The scope of the test should be clearly defined in the test plan. This lets you set reasonable test objectives that you can accomplish within the project schedule. Prioritize the scope based on risk.

> *"Besides the noble art of getting things done, there is the noble art of leaving things undone. The wisdom of life consists in the elimination of nonessentials."*
> —Lin Yutang

- **Test early and often.**

In this context, we are also considering reviews and inspections as static tests performed early in the project. Defects found at the end of a project (or even worse, in production) are costly, and they are a major contributor to project failure. Therefore, it makes sense to perform requirements, design, and code reviews to catch defects before they are built into the system.

- **Use techniques that leverage your time and resources.**

There are techniques that can help you deal with the infinite number of possible test case combinations. One very effective technique is cause-effect graphing based on requirements, which not only reduces the number of test cases, but also increases test coverage.

PLAN OF ACTION

1. Define a test process that includes risk analysis.

2. Develop test standards and templates that can be reused.

3. Base test estimates on measurable criteria, such as cases or requirements to be tested.

4. Build test cases to validate requirements or business processes, not random combinations of software functions.

5. Continually educate management that testing should be measured and estimated by fact, not guesswork or deadlines.

6. Keep a history of test measurements to help estimate future projects.

7. Continually streamline the testing process to make it more efficient and less time-consuming.

8. Consider using an automated test tool for repetitive tests once the test process has been defined and you know what you need to test.

CHAPTER NINE

CHALLENGE #4: TESTING WHAT'S THROWN OVER THE WALL

OVERVIEW

Traditionally, developers and testers don't talk to each other. When the developers are finished building a software program or system, they sometimes unceremoniously dump the product on the testers. This tendency is often called the "throw-it-over-the-wall" syndrome.

The assumption on the developers' side is that the testers will ultimately find all of the defects. This assumption leads the developers to test poorly, if at all. Because of weak testing, the testers often find that there are many defects in the system that should have been caught at the unit test stage by the developer.

In this chapter, we explore the root cause of "throwing stuff over the wall," which is primarily a breakdown of communication, and offer some ways to foster good communication between developers and testers. In addition, we discuss ownership and accountability, the role of test standards and processes, management support of testing at the developer level, and training developers to become excellent testers.

STATE OF THE PRACTICE

Randy Rice relates his experience: The only reason I am qualified to write or speak on testing topics is not that I have done all of these things perfectly, but just the opposite. I have tried many approaches to testing and have failed in some of those attempts. The good news is that failures can be turned into successes, as was the case on one project in which I was the leader of an independent test team. Our biggest problem was an assumption by the developers that we would test all of their work and find all of their defects. Moreover, my manager also had the same expectation.

After a few months of three people trying to test the work of twenty developers, we started to realize that something was wrong. My team and I were working overtime all of the time, trying to keep up with the software changes flowing through the independent test team. Often, we weren't sure what we were supposed to be testing because there were no written requirements for the changes. In addition, because of the heavy work load, much of our testing was superficial and therefore ineffective at finding the more severe defects. We knew as a team that we could not go on this way for much longer. Not only were we getting burned out, but we were not doing our job well. What could we do?

Our solution was to address several areas. First, we secured management support for the fact that our team could not keep up with the work and that the number of people was not the problem, the process was the problem. Management was behind us one hundred percent, which sent a message to developers that if there was a problem with a change, the testers were not to blame. Accountability rested solely on the developers. The second part of our solution was to reign in the scope of our testing. We made a policy of testing only moderately to highly critical changes. Third, we improved the quality of what we received to test. This meant that before we accepted any software changes for testing, we had to also receive a written set of requirements, a completed unit test plan, a complete description of everything affected by the change (such as programs, screens, databases, and so forth). Finally, we developed a set of test standards for test scripts and unit test plans, a unit and integration testing process, and a short, simple training course to teach developers how to plan and conduct a good unit test.

As you might expect, cultural resistance to this kind of change was strong. However, culture did not run the company; management did. Culture was something we had to change, and it did not happen overnight. After several weeks of ongoing training and communication from management, developers started to accept the new practices and found that the process had some good benefits, such as more reliable changes resulting in fewer night calls. The end result was a much lower defect rate (less than one percent of changes had to be reworked), more thorough testing, and a more effective test team that evolved into a true quality assurance function.

This experience contains several critical steps that are discussed in this chapter:

- getting management support to define roles and responsibilities
- establishing test standards and processes for developers
- establishing ownership and accountability at the developer level
- training developers to be excellent testers
- improving communication between developers and testers
- measuring and refining the processes
- establishing ground rules

IMPACT ON TESTING

From the preceding story, it should be apparent that the overall quality of testing had suffered from the following factors:

1. The initial level of defects coming into independent testing was high.
2. The testers spent much of their time identifying "nuisance" defects at the expense of testing critical test cases.
3. Independent testers had to perform more repeat tests because more work was handed back to the developers.

The overall negative effect of throwing stuff over the wall is that it wastes time and money. Rework is costly, especially when defects migrate to a later phase of software development, as in the case of moving from construction to testing. When defects are not caught close to the source of creation, people waste time sending the work back to the creator of the product. This cycle can escalate into so many loops that it seems the software will never see production. Unfortunately, it's the testers who usually get blamed for the delay.

There are other impacts on testing that are just as important as the economics of time and money. They include

- the level of communication between developers and testers
- the general attitude toward testing by both developers and testers

As we discussed in Chapter 4, independent testing can foster an us-versus-them culture that suffers from a breakdown of communication, a lack of trust, the physical separation of work groups, and a lack of understanding of what each group contributes to the overall project. Communication can also deteriorate over time simply because everyone seems too busy to talk. The attitude turns into one of "I'll do my job; you do yours."

When software is thrown over the wall to the testers, the attitude on the part of developers starts to become, "I don't have time to test, and besides, why not let the people who do testing best take care of it?" Meanwhile, the attitude of testers turns into frustration as they try to deal with whatever software comes their way.

SOLUTIONS TO THE CHALLENGE

Get Management Support to Define Roles and Responsibilities

This is the first and most important step. If management does not fully support a team approach to testing, chances are few that anyone else will. To get management support, you will need to make a persuasive case for the economics of a team approach to testing. The cost of rework is one issue. The cost of testing is another. You need to show how throwing stuff over the wall is costly due to the number of test/rework cycles, which tend to be greater when developers have no ownership or accountability in the testing process. Once you obtain management support, the message that sets the roles and responsibilities for testing needs to come directly from management to the organization, not from the independent testing team.

Establish Standards and Processes for Testing

A major step in solving the throw-it-over-the-wall syndrome is to build a process that specifies what testing the developers should perform and what testing the testers should perform. The issue is not whether independent testing is good or bad, but whether the right people are performing the right kinds of testing.

A very good way to define a process is to use the workbench model developed by the Quality Assurance Institute. This model, as applied to testing in Figure 9.1, is very simple, but it illustrates the essential parts of a testing process. The workbench is the domain of the person performing the work and can be used to highlight the process performed in any step

126

of the system development or maintenance process (requirements definition, system design, testing, and so forth). Input comes into the workbench and specific actions are performed on the input. A quality control step (represented by the "OK?" diamond) is then performed to ensure the process was performed correctly. If the quality control step is passed, output is produced and sent on to the next workbench, if needed. If the quality control step is not passed, the input is reworked and the cycle continues until acceptable output is achieved.

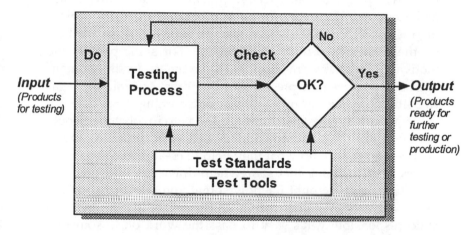

Figure 9.1: QAI's Workbench Model, Applied to Testing.

It is important to note that two very important resources support the workbench: standards and tools. We have already discussed the importance of tools, but have yet to address standards. Specifically, the quality control step should be supported by test standards, which may include unit test plan standards, test case standards, test script standards, and standards for any other items used in testing. Although standards evoke strong negative feelings in some cultures, test standards are essential to communicating the details of a process. Without standards, people are unclear as to exactly what is expected from them. On the other hand, many organizations have defined standards and processes, but fail to practice them even on an occasional basis.

Establish Ownership and Accountability at the Developer Level

It's one thing to have standards and processes, but it's another to make them a part of the daily work routine. To overcome the throw-it-over-the-wall syndrome, people must own the processes they use and be accountable for how they are performed. Without ownership and accountability, there is little upon which to build an effective process. Because ownership and accountability are attributes that indicate maturity, achieving them does not occur overnight. To establish these attributes, there must be a motivating factor. For some people, the motivation to follow processes might be the leadership of management, positive peer pressure, or the threat of avoiding negative situations, such as night calls or outsourcing.

A good way to establish ownership is to involve the people who will use the standards and processes in designing them. People tend to support what they help to create. Accountability comes from knowing that somewhere down the line, you will need to give an account for how something was done. When there is no accountability, there is no responsibility. Where there is no responsibility, it's easy to pass the work on to someone else—or in this case, to throw it over the wall.

Train Developers to Be Excellent Testers

After the test processes and standards have been defined and the adoption process continues, training developers in testing skills is the next most important activity. Training conveys a common understanding of how the standards and processes are to be applied. One of the most common objections to the application of test processes and standards in an organization is that each area is different and therefore cannot be standardized. Training in test processes and standards shows people how to apply a general process to a unique situation.

When developers are involved in the testing process, you will discover that instead of a few people testing the work of many people, many people are testing the work of many people. In addition, each person is doing the kind of testing that he or she is best suited to perform, and testing is not only effective—it is efficient.

Improve Communication Between Developers and Testers

Once you remove the wall between testers and developers, you are well on the way to an us-and-them—instead of an us-*versus*-them—culture. When the wall is down, developers and testers can communicate without one party feeling that the other is not doing its job. Amazing things start to happen. It has even been reported that when the wall is down, developers and testers start going to lunch together.

Communication improves because the testing process defines the testers' and the developers' roles and responsibilities. The same result of improved communication is characteristic of other areas of software development in which processes are defined.

Measure and Refine the Processes Continually

Two indicators of a highly mature process are measurements and continual process improvement. The challenge is to find the right things to measure and to avoid rewarding counterproductive practices. One of the more productive metrics is defect removal efficiency, which for a given phase of testing is the number of defects found in that phase divided by the total number of defects found during the life of the product (see Figure 9.2).

$$\text{Defect Removal Efficiency} = \frac{\text{Defects Found in Testing}}{\text{Defects Found During Life of Product}}$$

Figure 9.2: Defect Removal Effectiveness Formula.

Continual process improvement requires constant attention. Unless the process is very mature, an external force, such as a quality assurance group, is needed to keep the continual improvement process in motion.

Establish Ground Rules

One of the problems that can occur between developers and testers is a misunderstanding of test responsibilities. A way to deal with this problem is to establish ground rules that define the testing that each party should perform. Ground rules define what each party agrees to in the testing process. Should problems or disagreements surface, the ground rules provide a source for resolving the problems, and they carry more weight than if defined during the test.

SOLUTION IMPEDIMENTS

How do I overcome the skepticism over new process initiatives when past efforts have failed?

History is tough to forget and to overcome, whether it concerns testing processes or attempts to quit smoking. The important thing to remember is what the facts indicate: Quality software does not just happen by itself. Yes, there will always be those who are skeptical of trying to implement processes of any sort, but you must learn from past mistakes and keep going forward. The alternative is to keep testing low-quality software—and whatever else that gets tossed over the wall.

How do I convince management to take the lead in deploying processes?

The establishment of processes should be portrayed as a mission-critical task. The motivating force could be something negative, such as a project failure, a major public software defect, or the threat of outsourcing. A positive motivating force could be to gain a competitive advantage in the marketplace by becoming more efficient in software development.

What if the developers don't want to become better testers?

This is where management support is critical. If management is not willing to reinforce testing as part of the developers' job, then the developers are not likely to perform it. In addition, if management does not allow for expanded time estimates to allow for testing, developers will not test to the extent necessary for effective testing.

Besides securing management support, communicating the importance of testing is another key to success. You must emphasize the benefits of improved testing to the developers, using terms that are relevant. For example, better testing leads to fewer night calls or to fewer post-implementation fixes.

GUIDELINES FOR SUCCESS

- **People must be accountable for the products they produce.**

    "In order that people may be happy in their work, these three things are needed: They must be fit for it; they must not do too much of it; and they must have a sense of success in it."
    —John Ruskin

- **Management must build a quality culture.**

    If culture ruled the organization, everyone would show up at ten A.M. and there would be two-hour lunches. Cultural resistance is not an acceptable excuse for having poor processes. Management has the responsibility to put in place processes that will meet the objectives of the organization.

- **Test processes must be supported by test tools and test standards.**

  Without standards, the test process will be inconsistent; without tools, the test process will be inefficient.

- **Don't let your failures deter you from trying again.**

  "I think and think for months and years. Ninety-nine times, the conclusion is false. The hundredth time I am right."
  —Albert Einstein

- **Process deployment is a function of organizational maturity.**

  The more mature an organization becomes in following a process, the more fully processes can be deployed. Organizational maturity is more than just a matter of meeting certain criteria for an assessment—it is woven into the culture.

PLAN OF ACTION

1. Get management support for establishing clearly defined roles and responsibilities.

2. Establish test standards and test processes.

3. Build ownership and accountability into the test processes and standards.

4. Train people in how to apply the test processes and standards.

5. Continually measure and refine the processes.

CHAPTER TEN

CHALLENGE #3:
HITTING A MOVING TARGET

OVERVIEW

Change is a fact of life for all of us. Seasons change, people change, even our employment changes at an ever-increasing rate. For some reason, however, when it comes to technology, change makes even orderly processes chaotic. Just when you think you understand how to test a particular system or technology, the landscape changes, as if transformed overnight.

System requirements, if defined, are often the first things to change. In fact, in many projects, the system requirements may undergo constant change. On top of changing requirements, the software's operating environment may also experience significant change. Testers face the challenge of trying to test a continually changing system with criteria that don't always manage to change along with it. In past years, the question used to be, "How do you keep requirements from changing?" Now the question is, "How do you deal with changing requirements?" We understand and accept that we live in a changing world, but how do we control change and keep a grip on the product long enough to validate it? These are some of the questions we explore in this chapter.

STATE OF THE PRACTICE

The Big National Bank is in the middle of a four-year system development project called Project Infinity. The only problem is that the original scope of the project was two years. Because of changes throughout the project, it has been difficult to bring it to completion.

Some of the changes were unavoidable. In the first year of the project, a new federal law was enacted that affected the interest rates applied by the system. In addition, the hardware vendor for The Big National Bank announced that it will no longer be supporting the hardware used by the bank.

Some changes could have been avoided, but for political reasons within the bank they were accommodated. These changes included revised service charges for customers, a new product added by marketing to compete with a rival bank, and a special type of new technology for senior executives.

In addition to these changes, the developers decided to build the system using a newly acquired rapid application development (RAD) tool. Even though Project Infinity is a high-visibility project, the new technology was chosen as a way to build and deliver the system faster than using traditional methods and tools.

One major source of headaches is the amount of change that ripples through the system. Another factor is the rate of change. Every change to the system ripples through the development staff and onward to the independent testers. People are wondering if the tool that was supposed to make the project easier to build is actually making it harder to build; changes can be made with little regard to the rest of the system or for the people working with it.

The independent testers are becoming frustrated because every time they define a test plan, the software to be tested changes. The testers are having a difficult time keeping up with the developers. In short, everyone—developers, testers, users, and managers—is wondering if the name "Project Infinity" is prophetic.

This case study is typical of what many organizations experience as they try to build and deploy systems during times of rapid change. Some of the key themes in this case study include

- **Uncontrolled change from both internal and external sources**

  Some of the changes, like the new government regulations and the hardware support, could not be controlled. Other changes, like marketing the new product, were business decisions that could have been controlled but were deemed important enough to include in the project. In many projects, the changes are a mixed bag of unavoidable and avoidable changes. The challenge is to control the degree and impact of such changes.

- **Self-defeating technology that seems to be working against the project team**

  In this case, the RAD tool was used without a controlled process, and the team found it difficult to reach closure on the prototype. Prototyping is a good technique that has been used in other industries for many years, with great success, but the information technology team must learn from those other industries that the prototype is a working model that has to be replaced at some time. Otherwise, the system will never become stable.

- **The ripple effect of changes through development and testing**

  In some cases, a change might have very little impact on other areas of the system or business. In other cases, a change might have tremendous impact. The only way to tell what degree of impact a change will have is to perform an impact analysis using a RAD tool or a manual assessment. It is difficult in many cases to find all of the impact areas of a change, but at least some thought to the impact of changes is better than none.

Like a pebble dropped in a pond, a change can ripple through the system. This adds a challenge to testing, because what works well in isolation (for example, in unit testing) might fail completely when combined with other parts of the system (for example, during integration and system testing). Consequently, not only should you perform unit-level regression testing, you should also determine the degree of integration and system-level testing to perform.

- **Rapid development time frames that testers must try to match during testing**

   Developers can build software in RAD faster than testers can test it. In this case study, the issue is not only change, but the speed of change. This is another way that RAD tools can actually work against you if you lack a solid process in place to control development and testing.

   The speed of RAD tools also highlights the need for testing to be integrated in the development process. As a module is built and later changed, there should be steps in the process for the developer to perform solid unit testing. This kind of testing can be automated to ensure that the same basic test cases are executed to test each new version of the software.

IMPACT ON TESTING

Change is inevitable, and people should count on change occurring, rather than be surprised by it. We live in a world where change is occurring faster than ever. Businesses are being bought, sold, and merged; technologies are changing so rapidly that by the time a solution has been found, researched, and acquired, another technology has popped up to take its place.

The impact on testing is that although most of us like to take the time to plan a nice, orderly test, changes to the system come along like a sandlot bully, kicking down our sand castle. Developers and testers alike put time into designing their work, only to see it changed by circumstances beyond their control. Changes impact testing in the form of

- rework of testware, such as test scripts, test cases, and test plans
- regression testing of previously tested software
- backlog created by rapid change

Each of these impact areas reinforces how difficult it is to test a moving target. After all, the purpose of testing is to evaluate something based on a fixed set of criteria. What happens when the "fixed set" of criteria becomes a "fluid set"? Although it seems impossible to effectively test when everything changes, this is exactly the situation many people face.

To find the solutions to the problem of testing during rapid change, we need methods and tools that are fast, repeatable, and easily changed.

SOLUTIONS TO THE CHALLENGE

There are three basic methods for dealing with change:

- surrender to it
- track it
- control it

In the first method, you simply accept every change that comes your way. You may complain and get stressed out, but you are still at the bottom of the food chain.

In the second method, you as a bystander observe and keep record of changes, but you don't exercise control. You wind up with a lot of statistics, but chaos still reigns.

In the third method, you control the source of the change. In the context of a system project, a change control manager might freeze the system until the current version is implemented. In legacy systems, the change control manager might organize releases of software to control changes.

The optimal solution is to control the changes, instead of just tracking them or surrendering to them. This is easier said than done, but until changes are controlled, systems will be difficult and expensive to build. Even in the context of controlled change, the impact of change is still felt. Below, we address from the testing perspective the three major impact areas mentioned in the last section, and we offer solutions to minimize the impact.

Rework of Testware

Rework of testware should occur whenever the software changes or whenever new tests are designed. Because of this, test scripts, test plans, and test cases should be designed for change. Some ways that you can create *change-resilient* testware are as follows:

- **Use a template approach.**

  Templates for test plans, test scripts, and test cases can make changes easier. There are test management and test execution tools that allow you to fill in templates as needed. You can also design and create your own templates with a word processor.

- **Design a change mechanism into the testing process.**

  Your testing process should plan for and allow changes to be made easily. For example, a change-resilient testing process keeps test data in a separate location from the test scripts. This allows you to have a script for each process to be tested, but does not require a test script for each case to be tested. The difference in the total number of test scripts can be huge. If you are testing fifty processes and have ten thousand test cases, a change to the process would require you to change ten thousand test scripts if the test case information is contained in the scripts. If the data are contained in a separate test case file, you would only need to change fifty scripts.

The rule to remember is that every test item (script, case, and so forth) that you create is one more item you might need to maintain during the test.

- **Use a modular approach to test scripting.**

We discussed this concept in Chapter 8. Instead of having long, complex test scripts, either manual or automated, it is better to have short, simple scripts that can be combined to create a variety of unique tests. This helps reduce the amount of maintenance you might need to perform if the software changes.

Regression Testing of Previously Tested Software

Every time the system (hardware, software, peripherals, and so forth) is changed, there is a risk that a new defect will be injected or an old defect will be revealed. This is sometimes called the "I-just-changed-one-line-of-code" syndrome, and it has happened to the best developers. To illustrate how defects can be missed by only testing the change, let's look at Figure 10.1. In this figure, we are testing three test cases. In the first cycle of testing, test cases 1 and 3 pass, but test case 2 fails. We write up a defect report and the software is changed to fix the defect. In the second cycle of testing, we test only test case 2, which still doesn't work, so we write it up again. After the software is fixed, we perform another test cycle, which validates the defect is fixed.

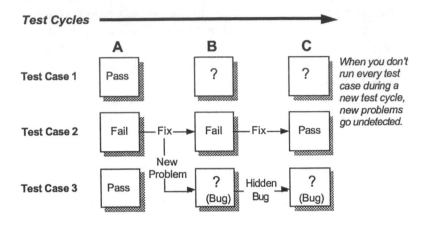

Figure 10.1: No Regression Testing (courtesy of Rational Software).

All three test cases have passed at least once during some point in the test, so the software is ready for production, right? Well, not really. Had we tested all three test cases in the second cycle of testing, we would have found that not only did the fix not work, it caused a new defect. In Figure 10.1, we didn't test all the cases, and the defect was missed.

Contrast this scenario with that of regression testing, shown in Figure 10.2. Regression testing is performed to ensure that the system works as correctly as before a change was made. In Figure 10.2, we test all cases in every cycle of testing. Because we perform the same test in all three test cycles, new defects are apparent—though they might be subtle. To perform true regression testing, you must be able to

- repeat a test or a series of tests exactly, repeatedly
- compare the results of testing exactly

Because of the precision required in regression testing, manual techniques fall short of achieving complete regression testing. In manual regression testing, there are simply too many chances for human error. Manual regression testing might be more accurately called *pseudo-regression* testing. This is an important distinction to understand, because many people *think* they are performing reliable regression testing manually. The result of this belief is a false confidence in the test results.

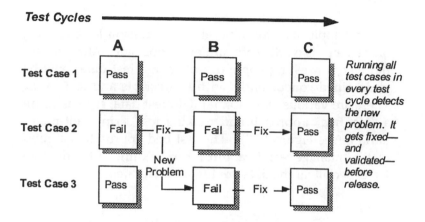

Figure 10.2: Regression Testing Performed (courtesy of Rational Software).

Automated testing is the only way to accurately perform regression testing, but there is much more to performing regression testing than just using an automated test tool. This is where the people and process aspect of testing come into play. Some common questions about regression testing issues follow:

- **How much regression testing is enough? If you change one line of code, must you regression test the entire system?**

This issue also applies to how much testing in general should be performed. The answer depends on the relative risk of the application and how many resources (testers, tools, environment, and so forth) you have available. If the risk is great enough, you will need to completely regression

141

test the entire system. Otherwise, you can get by with a lesser degree of regression testing, but keep in mind that regression defects can appear in very unexpected parts of the system.

- **How do you deal with data changed during a regression test?**

When people start thinking about regression testing, most of the focus is on the software execution side. After the initial test, however, people discover that test data must be maintained concurrently with test scripts and test cases. There are various ways to maintain test data, such as using a "test bed" approach and making test scripts self-maintaining (see Figure 10.3). The test bed approach is a good way to manage test data, but it can be difficult to administer, especially if the data are highly integrated.

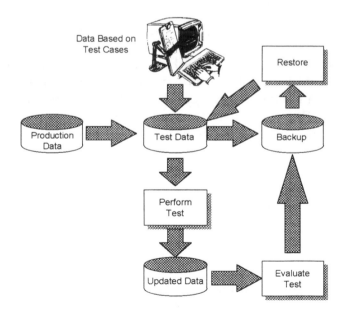

Figure 10.3: The Test Bed Process.

The concept behind a reusable test bed is that data files and/or tables are populated with a set or "bed" of data. The source of the data may be production data, created test data, or a combination of the two. A snapshot image of the data is then taken for backup and restoration purposes. Each time a test is run, data will be changed, but the test bed can be restored from the snapshot image. The test bed can also be continuously updated with data from new and modified test cases.

A test bed takes effort to maintain. For example, if your test cases are date-sensitive, you might need to perform regular updates of the test bed to meet test case criteria.

- **How effective is regression testing during rapid change?**

The effectiveness of regression testing depends on the kinds of tools you are using and the degree of change between the versions of the system under test. Some automated tools handle version differences, even major ones, rather easily, while other tools are a maintenance nightmare. The bottom line is that automated regression testing is essential and can be effective during rapid change.

However, in performing regression testing of systems that are greatly different, you may find that everything appears to be a difference. This kind of problem highlights the need for automated tools, especially for comparing versions of test results. Even the smallest difference can indicate a significant defect, but sometimes those small differences go unnoticed by human eyes.

Backlog Created by Rapid Change

In the traditional world, in which it took years instead of months to build a system, people thought in terms of one- or two-month system tests. With rapid application development, a new version of the software can be generated every day, but then testers do not have the luxury of performing a six- to eight-week test. So, what can they do?

The best solution is to automate testing, as described in Chapter 5. Even though automation is not the ultimate answer—because there are other issues to consider, such as defining the acceptable level of scope—trying to test RAD-developed software manually is no fun and can only be sustained for a short while before testers get burned out.

The increasing speed of development tools is a good reason to consider making testing an integral part of the development process. With RAD, you don't have much time to throw stuff back and forth over the wall.

SOLUTION IMPEDIMENTS

How do I test when my organization is changing at a chaotic rate?

You are not alone. Most software organizations in the United States operate in chaos mode. In fact, some people have actually bought into the idea that, in business, chaos is better than order. That's fine if you're a CEO, a business theorist, or a consultant, but if you're in the trenches, chaos can be a frustrating thing.

Management is responsible for running a business in a controlled manner. In fact, control is a core concept of management. As long as the chaos continues, so will the high levels of defects. The key is to make management aware of the situation, the risks, and the impact. Until things change, you can only do the best you can, which often means a scaled-down and unreliable test.

How do I find the time to perform impact analysis when changes occur so fast in my organization?

A starting point is to have the people initiating the change request perform an impact analysis. If the initiator is a business user, the impact analysis might focus on people. You can use a worksheet like the one in Table 10.1 to perform a people impact analysis. If the initiator is a technical person, the impact analysis can include affected system components. Both kinds of impact analysis should occur, so there might be a need for another person to assist.

Table 10.1.
People Impact Analysis Worksheet.

WHO'S IMPACTED BY SYSTEM	TYPE OF IMPACT	SIGNIFICANCE OF IMPACT	TEST STRATEGY TO ADDRESS IMPACT

The impact analysis should be part of the process and time should be allocated for it in the project estimates. Impact analysis and risk analysis are like testing in that if you don't have them in the process or allow time for them, they won't get done.

What if users become impatient with waiting for releases when they otherwise could have more frequent revisions?

If users are accustomed to getting changes constantly or whenever they want them, they might be reluctant to wait for the next release. On the other hand, if you can make the case that releases will lead to more reliable software, they might be willing (and even happy) to wait.

GUIDELINES FOR SUCCESS

- **Change will always be a part of our lives, so be prepared for it.**

    "Nothing endures but change."
    —Heraclitus

    "We must change to master change."
    —Lyndon B. Johnson

    "The very key to our success has been our ability, foremost among nations, to preserve our lasting values by making change work for us rather than against us."
    —Ronald Reagan

- **Change is occurring at an ever-increasing rate, so be aware of the risks.**

    "Change is happening faster than we can keep tabs on and threatens to shake the foundations of the most secure American business."
    —U.S. Congress Office of Technology

- **One small change can cause major problems.**

  "We believe that only 25 percent of AD [Applications Development] organizations perform regression testing, yet experience suggests there is a 50 percent chance that a modification to an individual program module will cause yet another problem or bug elsewhere in the application (0.7 probability)."
  —Brendan Conway[1]

- **Where change is concerned, control is everything.**

  "Inadequate configuration control is a key contributor to the problems of high maintenance costs, low quality, and low productivity. It is a very significant contributor to the problems of excessive time to market, long schedules, missed schedules, and cost overruns. Inadequate configuration control is an indirect contributor to low morale and low user satisfaction. Inadequate configuration control is also a barrier to eliminating the problems of low levels of reusable code and low levels of reusable design.
  "Inadequate configuration control is caused by inadequate capital investment, inadequate management curricula, inadequate software engineering curricula, and inadequate standards."
  —Capers Jones[2]

PLAN OF ACTION

1. Analyze your situation and find out where changes originate.

2. Establish a change control process that will manage changes.

---

[1] Brendan Conway, *Applications Development & Management Strategies Research Note*, August 24, 1994 (Stamford, Conn.: The Gartner Group), p. 1. Reprinted by permission.

[2] Capers Jones, *Assessment and Control of Software Risks* (Englewood Cliffs, N.J.: Yourdon Press/Prentice-Hall, 1994), p. 204. Reprinted by permission.

3. Make your testing processes change-tolerant by incorporating reuse and modularity.

4. Investigate how automated tools can help in your environment.

5. Explore the concept of scheduling changes in releases to control the process.

6. Add regression testing to your testing process.

7. Measure the number and impact of defective changes.

8. Use the information from the measurements to improve the maintenance and testing processes.

CHAPTER ELEVEN

CHALLENGE #2: FIGHTING A LOSE-LOSE SITUATION

OVERVIEW

Testers are often placed in a no-win situation. If they report that the software has defects and is not ready for production, they are seen as roadblocks to progress. On the other hand, if they certify that the software is ready for production and problems appear (as they often do), the testers are blamed for not being thorough enough in their testing.

This chapter addresses this lose-lose situation and proposes solutions that help testers communicate their role to the rest of the organization, identify what can reasonably be accomplished, and manage what customers can expect from production software.

STATE OF THE PRACTICE

It was the typical two weeks before the big deadline at ACME Software Company. Everyone on the project had been working extended hours to get the new version of the company's flagship product to market. People were stressed out and ready for some time off. It seemed like there was always one more thing to do before the software was ready to be shipped.

There was an urgency in meeting this deadline because ACME's competitor, AJAX Software, was also in the race to get its new and improved version to market ahead of ACME. ACME senior management had emphasized on several occasions the importance of getting to market first. Failure to do so would negatively affect the stock price and ACME's market share.

During this stressful rush to production, the testers on the project had been diligently performing a standard battery of tests. Each time a new build of the software was complete, the test set was executed. The only problem was that although the number of defects was decreasing, there were still serious defects in the software. Even the beta testers were negative about the overall quality of the software, and some had even removed it from their systems because it kept causing their systems to lock up.

The testers had conveyed this fact to the project team and to senior management consistently throughout the project, but the sense of urgency was not felt by everyone. In fact, one of the senior managers from the marketing area said, "We have done extensive research of our customers and have found that they are willing to tolerate a certain level of bugs. What's important is that we meet our commitment to our customers by getting the product to them on time. We can always release a follow-up Version 3.1 and even charge an upgrade fee." The testers just shook their heads as their status updates fell on deaf ears.

Finally, the day of decision arrived. After the final test of all standard test cases, there were still twenty-one major defects, eight defects that could be addressed with workarounds, and three defects that occurred so erratically that some developers swore they were due to sun spots. The test team collected its data and made the recommendation not to ship the software until the defects were fixed. When the test manager made this recommendation at the daily status meeting, you could cut the air with a knife.

Although the testers had some allies on the development team, most people were so tired of twelve-hour days that they just wanted to get the software out the door. The response from senior management ranged from ambivalence to anger, but the consensus was, "Thanks for the recommendation. Now go on to your next project, please."

Despite the objections from the test team, the software was shipped on time to stores and distributors nationwide. It didn't take long for ACME to start feeling the negative effects of the release. Many customers had experienced problems and were starting to return the product. ACME's technical support line was swamped with calls from irate customers. To make matters worse, the national press even publicized the story.

Naturally, this caused a panic at ACME. Not only were the customers angry, but the already stressed-out employees started quitting and the stockholders were threatening to sue. The crowning moment to this tale of woe was when the test manager was called into the director of marketing's office. "We just have one question," said the director. "We thought you were thoroughly testing this package. How could you have let it ship with so many defects?"

The test manager was speechless. The testers had gone on record so many times about the high levels of defects that she found it unbelievable that the testers would now be blamed for the problem. After thinking for a few seconds, she responded, "We didn't let the software ship. You did. You yourself told me that the customers would accept defective software. It seems that you took a business risk that didn't work out. I'm sorry you didn't take our recommendations, but I can't deal with this anymore. I quit."

In this story, the testers experienced the classic lose-lose situation. The testers were seen as an inhibitor to progress when they recommended a delay, but were also seen as lax when all of the problems occurred. No wonder so many QA and testing professionals resign in frustration!

It is true that people will tolerate a certain level of defects, but history has shown us two things: 1) the acceptable level of defects is an easy line to violate, and 2) the acceptable level of defects can quickly be reduced if a higher-quality product enters the market (as occurred when the Japanese automobiles flooded the U.S. market in the 1980's).

IMPACT ON TESTING

The lose-lose situation faced by testers has the effect of

- keeping an organization at a low level of process maturity
- trivializing and undermining the testing process
- demoralizing the testers
- fostering a false view of testing

Let's look at each of these testing impacts in detail.

Keeping an Organization at a Low Level of Process Maturity

When the testers are put into a lose-lose position, it is clear that the decision to place software into production is not driven by the process, but by circumstance. This indicates that the organization's culture is at a low level of process maturity, where it will remain as long as management's focus is on the product and not on the process, as discussed in Chapter 6 (see especially Figure 6.2 on page 83).

Instead of basing go/no-go decisions on circumstances at hand, management should rely on metrics and measurements of software quality. This is what the dashboard concept is all about, as was shown in Figure 6.1 (see page 82).

Trivializing and Undermining the Testing Process

In the case study, management chose to ignore the recommendation of the test team to delay implementation of the system, even in the face of severe defects. One must wonder why management bothered having people engage in the testing effort in the first place. When testing is seen as a roadblock to progress, it shows that people do not understand the role of quality control. Without controls in place, any kind of defect can pass through to the customer or user. In reality, when testing is an effective process, the end result is an efficient development process with reduced time-to-delivery.

Demoralizing Testers

Also evident in the case study was the frustration felt by the testers, who worked hard to find defects and contribute to the project. When the testers' recommendations were overridden, a message was sent to the testers that their work was just another piece of information.

Many testers feel personally responsible for the quality of the software being tested. However, there is no basis for this feeling of responsibility if they have no control over the creation of the software or the correction of defects. Without this control, testers are inspectors and are responsible for the identification of defects, not the quality of the software. In the case study, the testers did their job by finding the defects. It is hard, however, for people to disassociate themselves from the overall project.

Fostering a False View of Testing

The lose-lose situation implies that testers should be able to find every defect—without getting in the way while they are doing it. Lose-lose also puts the testing responsibility on one group of people and not on the entire organization.

The reality is that everyone on the project has a role in testing. Another fact is that most software is too complex to find all of the defects. There are some techniques that allow testers to find a very high percentage of defects, but there is always a chance that defects are lurking deep in the software logic.

SOLUTIONS TO THE CHALLENGE

Solving the lose-lose situation requires that you

- communicate the role of testing to the rest of the organization
- identify what testers can reasonably accomplish
- set and manage customer expectations of production software

Communicate the Role of Testing to the Rest of the Organization

It is essential that everyone in the organization knows the role testing plays. Otherwise, a false sense of security and responsibility will be placed on testing. Communicating the role of testing to the rest of the organization is an ongoing process that should be planned at regular intervals.

There are many lessons to be learned from the marketing profession in communicating the role of testing. These include the importance of repeated exposure and the emphasis on benefits, or, as mentioned before, WIIFM: "What's in it for me?" The communication of the testing role doesn't need to be intense, but events like learn-at-lunch sessions and other short venues can go a long way in making the message heard. Some teams have created one-page newsletters on a quarterly basis that are effective in communicating the role of testing.

Identify What Testers Can Reasonably Accomplish

There are more things to test than you will ever have time for, so it is very important that you determine what is reasonable to include in the testing process based on the risk involved and the resources available. A testing charter spells out the general boundaries of test responsibilities, who is responsible for testing, and the lines of reporting for a testing organization. Once the charter is complete, it should be signed by the test team and by management. The charter should then be distributed to the rest of the organization.

Set and Manage Customer Expectations of Production Software

In the strategic view of quality management (shown in Figure 6.1), the goal is to meet customer needs and expectations. However, until the customers' needs and expectations are accurately defined, the target will keep moving.

One of the best resources on how to manage customer expectations is Naomi Karten's book *Managing Expectations: Working with People Who Want More, Better, Faster, Sooner, NOW!* The following excerpt describes a real-life situation that illustrates how important it is for customers to understand your services.

On one particular occasion, we were making a critical and complex series of modifications to the system. To ensure adequate testing, we asked the customer manager to select some members of his department to serve as an acceptance testing team, and to send them to work in our department for the duration of the testing effort. Day one of acceptance testing arrived, and in walked the team selected for the task. It was clear from their attitude they wanted nothing to do with us. They'd do their job and be done with it. "Six weeks," they said, and they'd be gone.

Six months later, they were still with us. No, not because their projected six weeks of work took six months—it took three months—but the testing process worked so well that it wasn't disbanded at the end of the original test cycle. Instead, the team was assigned another set of changes to test, and then another. Finally, the acceptance testing team was formalized as a permanent team that reported to business management, but resided in our department and worked side by side with us.

What happened during the initial testing cycle was that our customers got a strong dose of the reality of doing systems work. They learned, firsthand, about designing transactions, running tests, dealing with malfunctions, and waiting for hardware outages to end. Although they didn't do any genuinely technical work, their proximity to our technical work had a huge impact on them. By observing us pulling our hair out while we debugged the errors they detected, they began to appreciate what our verbal explanations never succeeded in communicating: Systems work is complex and can't necessarily be done as quickly as customers would like.

The most valuable outcome of this experience was one we didn't anticipate: These customers became our mouthpiece to the rest of the organization. They showed up full of animosity toward us, yet by a month later they had become our strongest supporters. Previously, when we had tried to explain the intricacies of their requests, their management thought we were simply making excuses. Now, the acceptance testing team rose to our defense, and told their superiors, "Wait a minute, you don't appreciate what's involved."

It was almost comical; they began to sound *just like us.* The difference, though, was that now their management listened, and heard. We had become credible to customer management in a way we never would have on our own. And because their perceptions more closely matched our reality, their expectations of us became more reasonable.[1]

We have had experiences similar to those of Karten's acceptance testing team described above. In fact, at one organization, we have seen developers spend two weeks with the test team as interns. This internship was part of a cross-training initiative. The developers left the test team with a much better appreciation of what it's like to test software that has not been adequately tested beforehand. As in the above story, the developers who served as testing interns were some of the most vocal proponents of the testing process in the company.

---

[1] Naomi Karten, *Managing Expectations: Working with People Who Want More, Better, Faster, Sooner, NOW!* (New York: Dorset House Publishing, 1994), pp. 137–38. Reprinted by permission.

SOLUTION IMPEDIMENTS

What if communication of the testing role falls on deaf ears in our organization?

Until senior management gains a process focus, your message will not be fully understood. Until then, you can apply some of the principles we have discussed earlier in this book in raising management's awareness of testing, such as finding a champion in senior management and keeping up the communication. Management is not your only audience, however. Project teams, middle management, and peers also need to hear the message.

Sometimes, the toughest lessons are learned by experience. A project failure or other setback can sometimes get the attention of the organization.

What if management's expectations remain inordinately high, even though we've tried to explain the limitations to testing?

First, try to involve managers or their direct reports in testing activities, as described in Naomi Karten's story. People need to see firsthand what testers go through in designing and performing tests. Another approach is to use independent information, such as the *Scientific American* article referenced in the Related Reading section. This article points out the frustration in finding very elusive software defects in critical systems. If people think software testing is simple and can be performed completely in all situations, then they don't fully appreciate the magnitude and complexity of the job.

How do I set and manage expectations when our customers expect zero-defect software?

Randy Rice relates his experience: This reminds me of a case in which I advised my client, a software contracting company, not to promise zero defects on a particular project. A couple of weeks later, I was totally shocked when I learned that the contractors had very publicly promised to their customer's senior management that there would be zero defects in the software. The result was that the contractors could not deliver on the promise and the project failed. The main reason I advised them not to promise zero defects is that 1) in this case, there was a history of the customer changing its requirements, and 2) zero defects are difficult if not impossible to achieve in most situations.

In setting and managing expectations about defect levels, you need to address how defects will be defined and against what measure the system will be assessed. If a defect is defined as a difference from specifications or expectations, it will be nearly impossible to meet that standard. You can meet specifications that are well defined, but expectations will vary from person to person and can be affected by personal tastes and prejudices.

Without sounding like a proponent of defective software, you should set the expectation that defects will be very difficult to find and fix. In other words, never bet your job that all the defects are found. No matter how many test cases you define, you can define one more.

GUIDELINES FOR SUCCESS

- **Understand and communicate the role of testing and how it fits into the entire organization.**

> *"Quality is never an accident; it is the result of high intention, sincere effort, intelligent direction and skillful execution; it represents the wise choice of many alternatives."*
> —Willa A. Foster

- **Testing is more than one person's or one team's responsibility.**

  Each process should have points of quality control at each step of building software. The people responsible for building the product should also be responsible for controlling its quality.

- **It is incumbent on management to build a culture of trust and appreciation, not fear and blame.**

  "As a manager in your organization, you must start to behave in a manner that is congruent with the behavior you expect from your employees. The top managers in any organization must model the behavior they desire for the rest of the company."
  —Karl Albrecht

- **Our customers are our partners. They have a part in determining the quality of software they receive.**

  "Above all, we wish to avoid having a dissatisfied customer. We consider our customers a part of our organization, and we want them to feel free to make any criticism they see fit in regard to our merchandise or service. Sell practical, tested merchandise at a reasonable profit, treat your customers like human beings—and they will always come back."
  —L.L. Bean

PLAN OF ACTION

1. Develop a testing charter that defines the role of testing in your organization.

2. Publish the testing charter so that everyone in the organization understands what testing can or cannot accomplish.

3. Define testing processes and standards that facilitate the objectives outlined in the testing charter.

4. Deploy testing processes and standards.

5. Conduct training for the organization, including end-users and customers, on the details of the testing charter, testing standards, and testing processes.

CHAPTER TWELVE

CHALLENGE #1: HAVING TO SAY NO

OVERVIEW

The number one people factor challenge faced by testers is telling people that the software has problems. As a general rule, people do not like to hear bad news, and testers are frequently the bearer of bad news. Much like the couriers in ancient Rome, the testers sometimes pay a price for the bad news they bring. Fortunately, in today's business world, the bearer of bad news is not killed—but sometimes the punishment is a modern form of termination.

This chapter explains the ways in which testers present their results to management, developers, users, and customers. Then, we describe the problems that are associated with each of those presentation methods. Finally, the chapter suggests ways in which the problems found by testers can be presented in a constructive manner.

STATE OF THE PRACTICE

The first week of system testing was almost over, and the test team had already logged over one hundred defect reports. At this point, the system was not looking very good. Many of the initial defects were easy to find and should have been caught by developers during their unit testing. Unfortunately, the testers were trying to get their programs developed and testing was being shortcut to meet deadlines.

"Mary, this system is never going to fly," one of the test team members complained to her team leader. "Just look at all of these problems. If these are any indication of what the system is like, we're in deep trouble," the tester continued.

Mary agreed. "It isn't very encouraging. I think management needs to know about this."

So Mary wrote her weekly testing status report on the past week's testing. "The test team has serious concerns about the high number of defects found during system testing last week," her report stated. The report continued by stating that unless the situation improved soon, "the project would be in serious jeopardy."

When management and the project team read Mary's report, they were concerned and upset. Management was concerned that the project would not be ready to implement on time, and the project team felt they had been stabbed in the back with a negative report. One of the major problems that management had with Mary's report was that they did not know the exact nature of the problems, the number of defects found, or the best way to fix them. As one of the managers said, "Whenever someone comes to me with a problem, I expect to hear some solutions."

As the project continued, the defect rate did not level off until very late in the project, and even then there were still at least ten severe unresolved defects. When Mary delivered the final test report, the news was not good and neither was the reception. The project team felt that the testers were being overly negative, and management felt that there were not enough objective information and solutions in the test team's report. Because of this, management found the information from testing unconvincing, and it made the decision to implement the system anyway. The project managers made a convincing case that the severe defects could be resolved in production. What they didn't say was that it might take several months to accomplish.

The system went into production and the first three months of usage were torture for the customers, users, help desk staff, and developers. Every day brought more trouble reports and night calls. Eventually, many of the problems were fixed, but at a great cost to the organization. Some of the pain could have been avoided if management had been given more accurate test results and possible solutions.

IMPACT ON TESTING

When delivering test results, several approaches may be used. Some of these are highly effective, while others are not effective at all.

* **the informal approach**

   In this approach, test results are communicated by informal means. There is often no standard format for reporting. Sometimes, the report may just be a phone call or an e-mail message to the effect that "It works" or that "It's broken." It is an understatement to say that this method is dangerous for both the audience and the tester.

   For management, the informal approach lacks the data needed to make an informed decision on the state of the software under test. For the tester, there is no detailed documentation for protection if the software fails upon going into production.

- **the negative approach**

  In the negative approach to test reporting, the only news the test team can deliver is bad news. For a variety of reasons, some personal and some political, the test team may decide to be negative to prevent the system from going into production. This approach goes beyond objective information and seldom recognizes the positive aspects of the system.

- **the sugar-coated approach**

  In this approach, the positive results of the test are emphasized while the negative results are downplayed. Perhaps the test team is fearful of management's reaction to bad news, or they might not want to convey news that would make their friends on the project team look bad. This is a very dangerous approach because it builds a false confidence in the system's ability to work correctly in production.

- **the objective approach**

  This approach presents test results in specific and objective terms. The results may be expressed in numbers of defects found to date, the number of defects resolved to date, defects by severity level, and so on. In the objective approach, the information presented is accurate and objective, but may be delivered on an irregular basis.

- **the process-driven approach**

  In this approach, test reporting is defined by standards and by the testing process. Standards define the content categories, and the testing process defines when the report is produced. Since test standards define the content categories, measurements, and metrics, the results are consistent with those of the objective approach.

Of all of the processes described above, the process-driven approach works best at communicating regular and reliable results.

Test Reporting Is Your Friend!

To some people, test reporting is seen as a formality and is minimized. However, accurate and objective reporting of test results is the best way to protect yourself later. As we saw in the previous chapter, testers are sometimes blamed for software problems after the system goes live, even though they have warned people of problems. Test reporting is an excellent way of protecting yourself in this situation. You may still get blamed for defects, but at least the documentation will be on your side.

SOLUTIONS TO THE CHALLENGE

The solutions that follow are based on the process-driven approach to test reporting, since it is the most effective of those listed in the last section. It contains many of the aspects of the objective approach, but is a regularly occurring activity during testing.

Standardize Test Reports

Saying no is difficult enough without having to reinvent the way you say it every time. Test reporting standards help you deliver the news, both good and bad, consistently. The test reporting standard should define the format and content categories in the report. You can use published standards like those developed by the Institute of Electrical and Electronics Engineers (IEEE), or you can develop your own standards. See Figure 12.1 for a sample test report outline.

```
┌─────────────────────────────────────────────────────┐
│                                                       │
│  SECTION 1.  GENERAL INFORMATION                      │
│                                                       │
│       1.1      Summary                                │
│       1.2      Environment                            │
│       1.3      References                             │
│                                                       │
│  SECTION 2.  TEST RESULTS AND FINDINGS                │
│                                                       │
│       2.n      Test (Identify)                        │
│                2.n.1    Validation Tests              │
│                2.n.2    Verification Tests            │
│                                                       │
│  SECTION 3.  SOFTWARE FUNCTION FINDINGS               │
│                                                       │
│       3.n      Function (Identify)                    │
│                3.n.1    Performance                   │
│                3.n.2    Limits                        │
│                                                       │
│  SECTION 4.  SUMMARY                                  │
│                                                       │
│       4.1      Capabilities                           │
│       4.2      Deficiencies                           │
│       4.3      Risks                                  │
│       4.4      Recommendations and Estimates          │
│       4.5      Opinion                                │
│                                                       │
└─────────────────────────────────────────────────────┘
```

Figure 12.1: Sample Test Report Outline.

Make Test Reporting Part of the Testing Process

To ensure that test results are delivered regularly and at the right times, test reporting needs to be a part of the testing process. Just as test planning and execution should be defined in the test process, so should test evaluation and reporting. Test reporting can occur at any point in the testing process, from the very first inspection or review to the final user acceptance test.

Manage Your Audience's Expectations

Your test report has an audience of managers, developers, customers, end-users, and auditors. The people in these groups have their own interests and concerns, as shown in Table 12.1.

Table 12.1.
System Concerns.

Audience	Concerns
Managers	• The system will be delivered on time. • The costs of building and deploying the system are in line with projections.
Developers	• Meeting the deadlines management has set. • Starting the next project.
Customers	• Getting the system on or before the promised date. • Having a system that works.
End-Users	• Minimal disruption of their daily routine. • The system will make their jobs easier. • The system will work.
Auditors/ Inspectors	• Proper operational controls are in place. • Risk has been managed. • The system will work.

The problem with telling each of these groups no is that many times, more than just software quality is at stake. When software is critical to the success of business objectives, the potential business benefits are sometimes given a higher consideration than the risks of defective software. The customers and users reason that they are willing to live with a few problems to meet the business goals. The problem with this view is that the problems might be major.

Managing expectations for each of these audiences means communicating the role of testing and the risks of software failure. A healthy level of awareness is that software defects are costly and can put the business at risk. People need to understand that testers are paid to find defects and to report those defects. In fact, virtually the only time that testers can fail is when they fail to report the defects they observe.

People also need to understand that testers are not out to prevent the project from going into production, but are providing an essential part of the software development process—quality control. Without quality control, there is little to prevent serious defects from affecting people. Sometimes these defects can impact more than just business, they can affect human life.

Use Creative Reporting Techniques

Although different ways of presenting the bad news may not make it easier to deliver or receive, they can add interest and meaning to information. Charts, graphs, diagrams, and other elements aid in communicating test results. We live in a visually oriented society, and any marketing professional will tell you that it's the graphics that reach out and grab people's attention.

Focus on the Facts

Sometimes, a tester may be tempted to start grinding an ax when the overall level of defects in a system is high. You might want to write, "It's really, really bad," in your test report and leave it at that! The problem with doing that is, first of all, it sounds like you're whining; second, it sounds like you're just being negative; and third, people tend to ignore wheels that constantly squeak. The solution is to present objective information in your test reports, concentrating on measurements, like the number of defects found, unresolved, and resolved.

By the way, it's all right to be positive and point out the parts of the software that work. People need to be praised for their efforts. Just don't go so far in the positive direction that you present an unbalanced message.

Be Truthful

Sometimes, testers can get caught up in the push to get a project into production and can lose their objectivity. This happens especially when the project is delayed or extended and people start to experience burnout. Often, testers are afraid to confront management or make waves with development. This passive kind of testing is weak and ineffective, and is a sign that the testers and management do not understand the role of testing on the project.

When testers lose their objectivity or become passive, they tend to make most of the news good news. The story of the Emperor's new clothes contains a good analogy of what happens when nobody has the courage to tell management there are problems with the software. Or, consider the importance of truthfulness in a doctor's visit. Let's say that you notice a lump on your side and go to the doctor to have it examined. The doctor performs a biopsy and discovers that it is cancerous and should be removed immediately or your life will be at risk. However, let's imagine this doctor is having a problem telling you, so instead he says, "Oh, you're fine. Just go on home and it will be okay."

What would be your rating of the doctor's professional ability? Someplace between malpractice and gross negligence. Likewise, the tester who is not truthful in communicating the status of the software is not acting professionally.

Document Your Tests

People often forget that after a project goes into production, questions are sometimes raised about how the system was tested, what was tested, and what were the results of testing. In some cases, such as in regulated industries like medical devices, an inspector comes calling and will want to examine your test documentation. You will need to have some on hand!

In other cases, you may be visited by an internal or external auditor who will want to see evidence of your testing practices. You should be able to show your processes and the documentation from previous tests. If you produce software to sell commercially, you might be asked to provide evidence of test results before your marketing people can make that million-dollar sale. Think about it—if you have good test documentation, you're the hero; if you don't, you're the bum!

Another very useful kind of documentation is the post-implementation review. Some people call this the postmortem. The objective is to take a look back with 20/20 hindsight and document what went right and what went wrong on the project. You can also get an idea of how many early production defects were discovered. These production defects can help you measure your testing effectiveness. Your findings should be formulated into a post-implementation review report and kept on file to help document your continuous improvement process.

Build a Mature Culture

Just as it takes a mature person to accept the truth, good or bad, it takes a mature organization to accept the truth about a project. The question is, "How do we build a mature culture?"

Your organization can only mature as fast and as far as senior management matures. This means that senior management must move from a product focus to a process focus in order to see the first indications of improvement. There are other levels of focus after that, but most organizations would be dramatically transformed just by adopting a process focus.

The process focus is an important step because the product is no longer the issue. If bad news comes about, that's part of the process. If we can't deliver the product for another month because the defect rates are too high, that's part of the process. By focusing on the process, you remove many of the political influences that make the bad news hard for testers to deliver and hard for managers to accept.[1]

---

[1] The concept of process focus was promoted by Dr. W. Edwards Deming. He also has thirteen other points that will transform your organization. In the late 1980's and early 1990's, many companies were hot on the trail of Total Quality Management (TQM) as the cure-all for their quality problems. What happened to all of the interest in TQM? Some people suggest that TQM failed, but perhaps manage-

SOLUTION IMPEDIMENTS

What if my management only wants to hear good news?

If all management wants to hear is good news, then you need to question your role as a tester. If you cannot freely discuss the true status of the software you test, then the value of your work is minimized. First, work to change management's expectations of receiving only good news. Then, make a point of offering recommendations along with each problem you find. This keeps you from being seen as only a whiner and complainer.

How do we change the perception of testers as being negative?

One of the great things about a testing charter is that it spells out to everyone what your purpose is. Within the framework of a testing charter, you can work to build communication that is positive, yet objective. Let people know that you also want to see the project go into production on schedule, but that you are also charged with letting people know where the problems are. You can make this point in status meetings, written correspondence, and informal conversations.

How do I find the courage to say the system is not ready for production, even if my job is at stake?

This is the classic lose-lose scenario we discussed in the previous chapter, on Challenge #2. Although it is sometimes difficult to be the bearer of bad news, it is always better to live by your convictions. For example, after failures that result in the loss of life, investigators have often found memos and documents from engineers that reported unresolved problems.

---

ment failed to internalize the principles of TQM. People adopted TQM to the point of sacrificing profits and then it took a back seat. There are notable exceptions, in which organizations applied Deming's 14 points and succeeded in transforming their organizations into models of excellence, but these organizations are in a minority.

171

Even though these people might have suffered at the time for their honesty, they were vindicated later.

A bright spot for testers is the large demand for them in the information technology industry. You need to keep your résumé updated and your options open. Does this mean that you should change jobs just because people don't do things your way? No, at least not right away. Marketing your skills elsewhere should be considered if you realize you are in a dead-end situation, or if you can be held liable for consequences beyond your control.

How do developers decide whether or not to report defects found in a work in progress?

Most commonly, software is considered eligible for defect counting once it is ready for an inspection or an independent test. Although some developers "code a little, test a little," much like a writer reworks his own writing, counting defects too soon can skew your defect statistics and reduce the free flow of information between developers and quality assurance.

GUIDELINES FOR SUCCESS

- **Tell the truth, even if there are negative consequences.**

> *"Truth is incontrovertible; malice may attack it, ignorance may deride it, but in the end, there it is."*
> —Winston Churchill

> *"I would rather be trusted and respected than liked."*
> —Dr. Bobby Boyles

> *"If you don't stand for something, you'll fall for anything."*
> —Steve Bartkowski

- **Stick to the facts.**

  "Those who exaggerate in their statements belittle themselves."
  —C. Simmons

  "Just the facts, ma'am."
  —Jack Webb, *as Joe Friday*

- **Deliver a solution or solutions for each problem reported.**

  "Each problem has hidden in it an opportunity so powerful that it literally dwarfs the problem. The greatest success stories were created by people who recognized a problem and turned it into an opportunity."
  —Joseph Sugarman

- **Make test reporting part of the testing process.**

  If you want reporting to occur on a regular basis, it must be part of a larger process.

  "Communication is part of a process (either verbal or nonverbal) of sharing information with another person in such a way that he understands what you are saying. 'Talking' and 'listening' and 'understanding' are all involved in the process of communication."
  —Dr. H. Norman Wright

PLAN OF ACTION

1. Assess your current method of reporting test results and see if improvement is needed.

2. Develop test reporting standards.

3. Make test reporting part of the testing process.

4. Survey management, developers, customers, and users as to what information from testing they would find useful.

5. Set expectations of management, developers, customers, and end-users as to what information they can expect from test reports.

6. Explore creative ways to present test results using graphics, such as pie charts, bar graphs, and the like.

7. Improve the test reporting process by continually surveying management, developers, customers, and end-users to measure your effectiveness.

CHAPTER THIRTEEN

PLAN OF ACTION TO IMPROVE TESTING

The objective of a plan of action is to take you from where you are to where you want to go. There are two prerequisites: a baseline for measuring progress and a goal. The self-assessment in Chapter 2 guided you in gathering the quantitative data that support a true testing baseline. The challenges in Chapters 3 through 12 of this book have provided you with a basis for establishing your goals.

We believe that your goal should be quality, which has sometimes been described as a "race without a finish line." You need to establish goals, reach those goals, and raise the bar higher. However, goals should be realistic and achievable, not set to a level that seems unachievable to testers and may discourage them.

A plan of action is a road map for you to follow in improving. The plan of action must address the following components:

- Resources: the people, money, and technology needed to achieve your goal

- Schedule: the amount of time needed to achieve your goal
- People: the personal interactions that need to be addressed and resolved in order for you to achieve your goal
- Rewards: the organizational and personal benefits to be achieved by accomplishing your goal

There are two even more essential components of action: the will to take action and the way. This chapter addresses both. Unless there is a will to improve, the way will not succeed; conversely, having a determined will to improve without the way won't work, either.

BUILD THE WILL TO IMPROVE

Improvement involves change, and change involves risk. If testers continue to work the way they do now, they can expect the same level of performance. However, if the work processes are changed, there is a risk that the current level of performance will not be achieved. From our perspective, there are really two risks associated with improving testing:

- **Risk 1: The risk of failure.**

  Failure can come in many forms. It can be the failure that the change doesn't work, the failure that scarce resources will have been expended with no benefit, and the failure that the credibility of the individual proposing the change will be diminished. Of these, the one that people tend to fear the most is the loss of personal credibility.

- **Risk 2: The risk of not improving.**

  If changes are not proposed and tried, there is no opportunity for improvement. Without improvement, there is no hope that things will get better. Without hope, people tend to become demoralized. There is also the risk that other, more effective, people will step forward to perform the testing task, or that testing will be outsourced because another organization can do it significantly cheaper.

The assessment that an individual tester must make is: Which of the two risks am I most concerned about? Am I more concerned about failing, or about losing hope? Hopefully, the answer will be that the risk of lost opportunity (in other words, of lost hope) is much greater than the risk of failure.

There is a story told about Tom Watson, Sr., in his days as CEO of IBM. It appears that a senior vice president entered a new venture that involved the expenditure of about a million dollars. The venture was a complete failure, and the investment could not be recouped. Shortly after, Watson called the vice president into his office to discuss the venture. During the discussion, the vice president conceded that because of the failure, he expected to be fired. Watson quickly responded that he couldn't afford to fire the vice president because he had just invested a million dollars in his education.

Not all managers share the insight of Tom Watson, Sr. On the other hand, most managers know that if subordinates never fail, they are not trying hard enough to get better. Failure is one of the greatest learning experiences that an individual or organization can encounter. This is not meant to encourage excessive failure or to imply that employees who continually fail will retain employment; our intention is to put failure in the context of an ongoing improvement program.

To foster change, a manager should support improvement, provide the resources for reasonable plans of action, and then share responsibility with the individual for either success or failure. However, failure must ultimately reside with the boss, because it is the boss who controls most of the capability for improvement: the business resources, the right to reject or approve, the processes that will be used, and the motivation that will encourage or discourage the individual to push to succeed.

The individual initiating change must identify an opportunity to improve by knowing the current baseline and having a goal, and then must step forward with a plan of action for improvement. That person must be willing to play a game of "You Bet Your Job!" The rules of the game are simple, as follows:

- The individual must believe that change is needed and that the plan of action being proposed will accomplish that change.
- The change must be in the best interest of the organization.
- The individual must not be concerned about personal credit for the improvement.
- The individual must be enthusiastic about the change.
- The individual must be committed to working hard to make the change happen.
- The individual must be extremely strong and positive when presenting the proposal to the boss, and if it is rejected, must be willing to rework and repropose the idea until it is accepted.
- The individual must have sufficient confidence in his or her abilities that losing a job and acquiring a new job does not appear as an insurmountable challenge.

The key to the will for change is seated in the confidence in one's ability to recognize the need for change and in the capability to propose and implement that change. It is amazing what an individual can do with the will and the way to cause change to happen.

USE THE WAY TO CHANGE THE TESTING PROCESS

Change is a process, not an idea. Many great ideas are not implemented because no action is taken. A process to initiate change causes action to take place. The process shows people what steps need to be taken in order to make change occur. It would be nice to say that change is as simple as 1, 2, 3, but in our opinion it is a little more complex: It's as simple as 1, 2, 3, 4, 5, and 6. The six-step way to make change happen is illustrated in Figure 13.1.

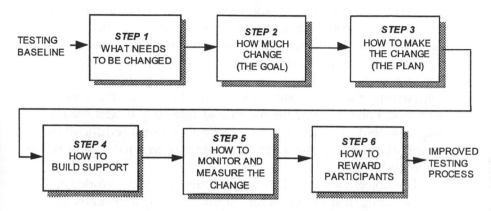

Figure 13.1: The Way to Make Change Happen.

As shown in the figure, the six steps begin with the testing baseline (see Chapter 2), which identifies opportunities for improvement. Step 1 determines which of the changes appear to be most promising. Step 2 determines how much change will occur by establishing a goal relative to the baseline and showing the gap to be closed by the change. Step 3 requires developing a plan to make the change. Step 4, one of the most important steps in that it is the people step, builds support and gains the assistance needed to make the change. Step 5 monitors and measures the rate of improvement from the baseline to the goal, and when that rate of change is not meeting the plan, makes adjustments accordingly. Step 6 is also an important step in that it rewards the people for making the change. Reward is a key step in that it recognizes the individuals who have taken a risk to make the change occur, and equally important, encourages them to make more changes. The output from the six-step process is an improved testing process. The six steps are individually discussed below.

Step 1: What Needs to Be Changed

Establishing a software testing baseline is very important in targeting testing activities for improvement. The baseline can indicate which activities consume excess time, which activities are performed least effectively, and which activities are subject to the most rework. Also, without the baseline, it is difficult to set realistic improvement goals or to measure improvement.

There are two methods that can be used to select activities for improvement. These are the subjective method and the objective method. The subjective method relies on the experience and knowledge of the individual selecting an activity for improvement. This process can be effective, but it is difficult to defend the results against different opinions on what should be improved.

The objective method uses a selection process. Worksheet #1: Selecting Test Activities for Improvement is a recommended objective method for selecting improvement candidates. This method uses the following three criteria as the basis for selecting an improvement candidate:

- Management Support: The selected test activity would receive management support. The support would be based on the ability of the improved activity to better drive the IS organizational mission.
- Probability of Success: The improvers would have the necessary skill, motivation, and resources needed to implement the improvement successfully.
- Potential Payback: The benefits that would be derived from having the change implemented successfully.

The worksheet is completed by performing the following tasks:

- Task 1: List the candidates for improvement that are identified through baseline analysis or recommendations from involved parties. Note that the test activities involved as potential candidates should not be exces-

Worksheet #1: Selecting Test Activities for Improvement.

#	IMPROVEMENT CANDIDATE	CURRENT BASELINE	SCORE 1-5 1 = very little / 5 = very much			TOTAL SCORE	GOAL
			Management Support	Probability of Success	Potential Payback		

sive in number, meaning that the process of identifying candidates should eliminate those that have little probability of success or little payback.

- Task 2: Identify the current baseline for each improvement candidate. This requires identifying one or more metrics that will be used to quantify the baseline.
- Task 3: Score each of the three selection criteria for each improvement candidate. Rate them from 1 to 5, with 1 being very little, 3 being average, and 5 being very much. For example, in the area of management support, 1 would indicate very little management support and 5, very much management support.
- Task 4: Select the best improvement candidate by totaling the score for the three criteria and putting it in the total score column. The improvement candidate with the highest score should be chosen for improvement, subject to reasonable judgment.

The individual or group responsible for improving the test process can select one or more improvement candidates depending on the level of management support, the amount of resources available for improvement, and the need for rapid improvement.

Step 2: How Much Change (The Goal)

This step determines how much improvement will be recommended by establishing an improvement goal. The goal should use the same metrics used for the baseline, so that the gap between the baseline and the goal will indicate the level of improvement to be achieved.

There are many theories of goal-setting. We believe that goals should be realistic and achievable within a reasonable period of time. It appears more appropriate to us to establish a series of escalating goals rather than establishing one stretch goal for which the probability of success is low, even though the latter does encourage people to reach for more than they believe is achievable. We recommend something like the Japanese concept of Kaizen, a never-ending process of ever-increasing, higher goals. Your goal, once established, should be recorded on Worksheet #1.

Step 3: How to Make the Change (The Plan)

It has frequently been said that the failure to plan is a plan for failure. Planning does not have to be a complex or lengthy process; it merely means identifying what needs to be done in order to achieve success.

Worksheet #2 is an improvement plan for the technical components of change. The technical part of the plan is differentiated from the people part, which will be addressed in Step 4.

Completing the technical improvement plan requires the following:

- Selected Improvement Name: the name of the plan for improving the chosen candidate identified on Worksheet #1
- Selected Improvement Description: a brief description of the improvement
- Plan to Achieve Improvement:

    a) Step Number: the sequence number of the step
    b) Step Name/Description: the reference name and brief description of the step
    c) Implementation Responsibility: the name of the individual or group that will be responsible for performing the step
    d) Dates: the proposed start and stop dates for the step
    e) Other Resources: the resources that will be needed for implementation of the step

Step 4: How to Build Support

People make things happen; people stop things from happening. Viewing change exclusively as a technical problem is a

183

Worksheet #2: Technical Improvement Plan.

STEP NUMBER	STEP NAME/DESCRIPTION	PLAN TO ACHIEVE IMPROVEMENT				
		IMPLEMENTATION RESPONSIBILITY	DATES		OTHER RESOURCES
			START	STOP	

SELECTED IMPROVEMENT NAME:

SELECTED IMPROVEMENT DESCRIPTION:

mistake. The change can be highly desirable, the plan well laid out and achievable—yet still one or more people don't want it to happen. When change becomes a political issue, the challenge of success is significantly increased and the probability of success is substantially reduced.

For any change activity, the individuals who have a vested interest in that change, whether positive or negative, will fall into one of four categories:

- Make it happen: the people who are personally willing to lead the effort to make the change.
- Help it happen: the people who will work to make the change happen, but will not take a leadership position.
- Let it happen: the people who do not care whether or not the change occurs, and will neither help nor try to stop the change from happening.
- Stop it from happening: the people who will take an active position to stop the change effort. The stop-it-from-happening people can be one of two types. There is the overt individual who formally announces he or she doesn't believe the change should occur. These people are honest and can be dealt with. The other type consists of those who appear to support the change, but in fact try to sabotage it in any way possible—for example, a manager who ostensibly supports the change but will not allocate any resources to make it happen.

This step involves identifying the participants in the change process. The participants are not only those who work at making the change happen, but those who have a vested interest in the success or failure of the change. For any change, this would rarely ever exceed twenty people, and for smaller changes, may be only five to seven individuals.

Worksheet #3: People Role in the Improvement Plan can be completed by performing the following tasks for each of the columns, respectively:

- Participants: Identify those who have a vested interest in the change, including those who will need to be involved in making the change happen.
- Where Now: Identify where the individual now stands by putting the individual in one of the four categories: make it happen, let it happen, help it happen, or stop it from happening.
- Where Needed: Determine which of the following three categories the individual must be involved in: make it happen, let it happen, or help it happen.
- What Role: Determine the role that each participant must take. The role must be as specific as possible so that a plan can be developed to ensure that the individual fulfills that role.
- How to Get Where Needed: Use the plan to determine how to move the individual to where he or she is needed.

Step 5: How to Monitor and Measure the Change

What gets measured gets done. Managers of change need to know rates of progress, and when goals have been achieved. While it is nice to undertake a project and declare success, that success can be challenged without appropriate quantitative data to back up the success statement. The objective of Step 5 is to establish the monitoring and measuring processes for implementing the change.

For small changes, monitoring and measuring may only occur at the time the change is implemented. For larger changes, it may be desirable to monitor and measure at various points throughout the improvement process. The change manager needs to make the decision as to how frequently progress should be monitored and measured.

Worksheet #4: Measurement and Rewards provides the basis for the monitoring and measuring activity. This worksheet contains the following monitoring and measuring data:

- Selected Improvement Name: the name of the improvement candidate selected from Worksheet #1.

Worksheet #3: People Role in the Improvement Plan.

PARTICIPANT(S)	WHERE NOW	WHERE NEEDED	WHAT ROLE	HOW TO GET WHERE NEEDED

- Measurement:

  a) Baseline: the baseline prior to making the change as recorded on Worksheet #1.
  b) Goal: the goal for improvement as recorded on Worksheet #1.
  c) Metric(s) to Measure Improvement: the metrics that were selected for use in the baseline and goal.
  d) How Data Will Be Collected: the process that will be used to collect the quantitative data for the metric(s). This should be specific and should address areas of reliability of data collected.
  e) Who Will Collect/Monitor: the name of the individual responsible for monitoring and measuring improvement.

Step 6: How to Reward Participants

Bill Perry relates his experience: I remember one supervisor telling me early in my career that I was rewarded every week for my work, when I received my weekly paycheck. I also remember reading theories on managing people, which indicated that money was never a motivator, but the lack of it was a demotivator. In other words, giving me an annual raise would not motivate me day after day to perform in an outstanding manner. That motivation must come from a source other than money.

One of the management principles that I learned very early in my career as a supervisor was that you could not thank people often enough. Of all the things I was criticized for as a supervisor over the years, I was never criticized for thanking an individual. I also learned that it was important to thank people in a variety of ways. This was because you were never sure how people wanted to be rewarded. Some people want a written thank you that they can take home to show to their family. Others want to be recognized in front of their peers. Still others want to be thanked in private. Some want a tangible thank you, such as a certificate, plaque, or small gift. I learned that even when I did any of these things, no one complained.

Anyone initiating change is a risk taker. People need to be rewarded for taking risks, not punished. It is even desirable to thank people for taking a risk, even though the desired change did not occur.

Some managers like to use rewards as something to work toward. For example, if a team successfully implements a change, the reward may be a complimentary lunch off premises with the boss. Having people know the reward ahead of time may motivate them. Other managers like the reward to be a surprise, after the fact.

What's important is that people are rewarded. Even if that reward is only a simple thank you. However, thank you's are best given either at an individual's workstation or at an open forum when that individual's peers are present. Change is not complete until the participants are rewarded. Worksheet #4 provides a place to indicate the recommended rewards for the participants in the change.

TESTING IMPROVEMENT IS A NEVER-ENDING PROCESS

World-class testing organizations are those that continuously undergo improvement. It is in striving for excellence that innovation occurs. When testing organizations are just performing testing tasks, they are not properly challenged to excel. It is only when individuals push themselves to be the best of the best that they find ways to accomplish what seem to be impossible goals.

This book has stressed that the major challenges facing testers are people-oriented. Much of the book has emphasized the relationships between the testers and the parties involved in testing. This last chapter has emphasized the relationship between the tester and the testing process. People issues are central to these relationships, and they present testers with the most exciting and challenging parts of their careers in testing. Now that you have had the opportunity to explore these issues, it's time to take action.

Worksheet #4: Measurement and Rewards.

SELECTED IMPROVEMENT NAME:

MEASUREMENT:

A) BASELINE

B) GOAL

C) METRIC(S) TO MEASURE IMPROVEMENT

D) HOW DATA WILL BE COLLECTED

E) WHO WILL COLLECT/MONITOR

REWARDS

PARTICIPANT	REWARD IF GOAL ACHIEVED

RESOURCES

RELATED READING

Brooks, Frederick P., Jr. *The Mythical Man-Month: Essays on Software Engineering.* Reading, Mass.: Addison-Wesley Publishing, 1978.

Conway, Brendan. *Applications Development & Management Strategies Research Note.* Stamford, Conn.: The Gartner Group, August 24, 1994.

Covey, Stephen. *The 7 Habits of Highly Effective People.* New York: Simon & Schuster, 1989.

DeMarco, T., and T. Lister. *Peopleware: Productive Projects and Teams.* New York: Dorset House Publishing, 1987.

Freedman, D.P., and G.M. Weinberg. *Handbook of Walkthroughs, Inspections, and Technical Reviews,* 3rd ed. New York: Dorset House Publishing, 1990.

Gause, D.C., and G.M. Weinberg. *Exploring Requirements: Quality Before Design.* New York: Dorset House Publishing, 1989.

191

Humphrey, Watts S. *Managing the Software Process.* Reading, Mass.: Addison-Wesley Publishing, 1990.

Jones, Capers. *Assessment and Control of Software Risks.* Englewood Cliffs, N.J.: Yourdon Press/Prentice-Hall, 1994.

Keyes, Jessica, ed. *Software Engineering Productivity Handbook.* New York: McGraw-Hill, 1992.

Littlewood, B., and L. Strigini. "The Risks of Software." *Scientific American* (November 1992), pp. 62–75.

Mosley, Daniel J. *The Handbook of MIS Application Software Testing.* Englewood Cliffs, N.J.: Prentice-Hall, 1993.

Perry, William E. *Effective Methods of Systems Testing.* Reading, Mass.: Addison-Wesley Publishing, 1995.

Weinberg, Gerald M. *Quality Software Management, Vol. 3: Congruent Action.* New York: Dorset House Publishing, 1994.

CERTIFICATION PROGRAMS FOR SOFTWARE TESTING

Certified Software Test Engineer (CSTE)
Quality Assurance Institute
7575 Dr. Phillips Blvd., Suite 350
Orlando, FL 32819
Phone: (407) 363-1111
Fax: (407) 363-1112
Web: http://www.qaiusa.org

LOCAL QUALITY ASSURANCE GROUPS

The following groups are affiliates of the Quality Assurance Institute Federation (in order by city, country, or continent). The purpose of these affiliates is to create a network of resources to use in fostering your personal knowledge of IT quality assurance. If you are interested in an existing group, you may call QAI at (407) 363-1111 to find out contact information for the group nearest you.

United States

ATLANTA, GA
Atlanta Quality Assurance Association (AQAA)

AUSTIN, TX
Austin Association of IT Quality Professionals (AA-IT-QP)

BALTIMORE, MD
QA Association of Maryland

CHICAGO, IL
Chicago Quality Assurance Association (CQAA)

COLUMBUS, OH
Central Ohio QA Association

HARTFORD, CT
QA Association of Connecticut (QAAC)

KANSAS CITY, MO
Kansas City QA Association (KCQAA)

LONG ISLAND, NY
Long Island Association of Quality Improvement Professionals (QIP)

LOS ANGELES, CA
Southern California QA Association (SCQAA)

MINNEAPOLIS/ST. PAUL, MN
Twin Cities QA Association

MORRISTOWN, NJ
New Jersey Quality Assurance Association (NJQAA)

NEW YORK, NY
Quality Management Association (QMA)

ORLANDO, FL
Quality Assurance Association of Central Florida (QAACF)

RALEIGH, NC
Triangle Information Systems Quality Association (TISQA)

SALT LAKE CITY, UT
Salt Lake City QA Association

SAN FRANCISCO, CA
Bay Area QA Association (BAQAA)

SEATTLE, WA
Seattle Area Software Quality Assurance Group (SASQAG)

ST. LOUIS, MO
St. Louis QA Association (SLQAA)

WASHINGTON, DC
Washington D.C. QA Association (WDCQAA)

CANADA

MONTREAL, PQ
Association Quebecoise d'Assurance Qualité Informatique

OTTAWA, ON
Association of Quality in Software Engineering of Ottawa (AQO)

TORONTO, ON
Toronto Association of Systems Software Quality (TASQ)

OTHER COUNTRIES AND CONTINENTS

AUSTRALIA
Bergman Voysey & Associates (Sydney)

EUROPE
Quality Forum

RUSSIA
Russian QA Association

SOUTH AFRICA
South African Society for Quality (SASQ)

INDEX